D0209156

What Is COMMUNITY JUSTICE?

What Is COMMUNITY JUSTICE?

Case Studies of Restorative Justice and Community Supervision

WITHDRAWN

David R. Karp
Skidmore College

Todd R. Clear
John Jay College of Criminal Justice

Editors

Sage Publications
International Educational and Professional Publisher
Thousand Oaks ▪ London ▪ New Delhi

HV
9304
.W45
2002

Copyright © 2002 by Sage Publications, Inc.

All rights reserved. No part of this book may be reproduced or utilized in any form or by any means, electronic or mechanical, including photocopying, recording, or by any information storage and retrieval system, without permission in writing from the publisher.

For information:

Sage Publications, Inc.
2455 Teller Road
Thousand Oaks, California 91320
E-mail: order@sagepub.com

Sage Publications Ltd.
6 Bonhill Street
London EC2A 4PU
United Kingdom

Sage Publications India Pvt. Ltd.
M-32 Market
Greater Kailash I
New Delhi 110 048 India

Printed in the United States of America

Library of Congress Cataloging-in-Publication Data

What is community justice?: case studies of restorative justice and community supervision / edited by David R. Karp and Todd R. Clear.
       p. cm. —
Includes bibliographical references and index.
  ISBN 0-7619-8746-0 (pbk. : alk. paper)
  1. Community-based corrections—United States—Case studies. 2. Alternatives to imprisonment—United States—Case studies. 3. Criminal justice, Administration of—United States—Citizen participation—Case studies. I. Title: Case studies of restorative justice and community supervision. II. Karp, David R., 1964- III. Clear, Todd R.
  HV9304 .W45 2002
  365'.6'0973—dc21

                        2001005423

 01   02   03   04   05   10 9 8 7 6 5 4 3 2 1

Acquiring Editors: Stephen D. Rutter and Jerry Westby
Editorial Assistants: Kirsten Stoller and Vonessa Vondera
Production Editor: Claudia A. Hoffman
Copy Editor: Barbara Coster
Typesetter/Designer: Denyse Dunn
Indexer: Molly Hall

Contents

Preface

This book began as a research study funded by the Edna McConnell Clark Foundation in 1998. We had both recently written about community justice as a idea and had visited several promising programs around the country. We wanted to know of other programs that existed and conducted a nationwide survey of probation programs. Although we discovered many, we chose to focus our attention on just a few—some of which seemed to capture many of our ideas about community justice and others that developed one or two aspects of the model with great initiative and focus.

We very much see this book as the third in a trilogy of our work on community justice. The first, *Community Justice: An Emerging Field*, collected a series of new and previously published scholarly articles that addressed the core themes of community justice. Although few of the articles used the term community justice, it was apparent that a coherent literature was developing under this rubric. The second, *The Community Justice Ideal*, clarified the philosophical underpinnings of community justice and provided a coherent statement of the approach. This book follows from the previous two by providing a series of case studies—real-world programs that attempt to fulfill one or more core elements of the community justice model.

We offer these case studies not as comprehensive descriptions of the emerging idea of community supervision but as illustrations of the kind of change that is underway. As you read the selections in this book, consider how the values of community supervision reflect the new idea that offender supervision is not just about criminal justice but is concerned with community justice. These new approaches tailor their efforts to fit the particular needs of the communities they serve, and so they become not rote community supervision functions but important new strategies for improving community life.

These six case studies thus illustrate, as we have said, new ways of doing business. Read them with an open mind but also with a critical eye. Their stories are interesting but raise important questions, just as they stimulate new thinking. What do you think about this new way of doing business? What are the likely problems that arise from change? How long will these innovations last? What issues do they raise that, eventually, will have to be addressed?

These illustrations do not describe programs or approaches that are perfect. They are as infused with the energy and enthusiasm that comes with innovation as they are afflicted by lapses and problems that always come with important changes. There are no perfect answers to the problems facing community supervision today, but there are fascinating and encouraging possibilities contained within the ideas illustrated by the selections in this book. We hope you will be stimulated by the descriptions of innovation.

Most of all, ask yourself the following: Do you find these new approaches to be exciting, and do they inspire you to become involved in building the new frontier of community supervision?

— *David R. Karp*
— *Todd R. Clear*
January 2002

The Community Justice Frontier: An Introduction

It is not rare for offenders to be in the community. This year, more than 3,500,000 probationers are serving misdemeanor or felony sentences in the community. An additional 600,000 former prisoners will be released into the community, either under some form of supervision or outright, with no strings attached. Another 7,000,000 people will be released from jail. These large numbers of offenders in the community compare to the 2,000,000 who are in prison or jail (Bureau of Justice Statistics 2001). So although it is typical that when we think of corrections, we think of the prison, in fact, it is far more important to consider the role of community supervision of offenders when we think of the penal system in its entirety.

The history of community supervision of offenders is a relatively new one. Probation is barely a century old, and parole is half again that age. Although they each apply to identified offenders who are allowed to be in the community, they have historically quite different rationales. Probation was developed as a form of leniency, a "second chance" for selected offenders who might be inclined to reform without the need for an onerous prison sentence. Parole, on the other hand, was devised as both an incentive for prisoners to use their time in prison well, so they could earn an early release, and an option for dealing with some offenders who, it was thought, should be given an opportunity to show that they could live crime-free in the community.

For most of this history, and despite the differences in original justifications, corrections in the community has followed a fairly dependable path. The dominant mode of supervision was some form of "casework," in which a representative of the community supervision agency—an "officer" or "agent"—would regularly see the ex-offender, provide structured advice or guidance on what to do, and gather the information necessary to reassure authorities that the "client" was making a successful adjustment to the community. The idea was that the officer (or agent) would be given a caseload of offenders, who would receive various levels of control and support (based on need) on a one-on-one basis.

Within this "caseworker" model, there were many innovations and technical advances. Some agencies experimented with the use of very small caseloads, so that "intensive" supervision might be used to improve offender adjustment to the community. In recent years, systematic classification systems have been devised to identify those clients who need the most attention and to help the supervision officers home in on the most important tasks to undertake with those clients. Detection devices have been enhanced: electronic monitoring of offenders' whereabouts help the officers know if the rules of community supervision are being obeyed, and regular drug testing provides reliable information about substance use. Increasingly, specialized supervision methods have been devised to deal with high-priority cases such as sex offenders, addicts, and the mentally ill. The last generation of innovation in community supervision has been particularly focused on these kinds of improvements.

After a century's work of experimentation and innovation within the caseworker paradigm, there is much reason to doubt the value of this approach. Studies of intensive supervision, carried out over a 30-year period, have shown that the method does not reduce recidivism but appears actually to increase it. The new control technologies have increased the distance between the officer and the offender in the community and have contributed to an atmosphere in which they seem to be increasingly at odds with each other. Some evidence seems to support the use of systematic behavioral treatments, but there is an equally strong indication that these effects are small, and by far most offenders are not exposed to these approaches. At the same time, the morale of community supervision workers has seemed to be reaching an all-time low, and studies of burnout and cynicism prevail in the literature.

There is more bad news. Caseloads have grown for 50 years, and it is not uncommon for an officer to carry 100 or more clients. In these settings, officers feel they have little time for more than basic monitoring of the client's conduct, and the pressure for accountability sometimes creates a feeling of deep frustration for staff. Ironically, the recent changes in caseload management policies have been associated with an increase in failure rates of clients under supervision. The system seems to focus on routines of surveillance without much emphasis on services, and relationships are impersonal in the face of bureaucratic routines. Public confidence in community supervision is not very high, and public attention seems regularly drawn to failures of the system rather than its successes.

In this way, it seems not overly dramatic to say that community supervision stands at a crossroad. A century of work within the dominant paradigm has not provided much in the way of results. Yet, the weight that should be given to the community supervision function, with the large number of offenders living and working in the community, has never been so high.

These are all reasons why, among the creative leadership in community supervision agencies, there is a murmuring of dissatisfaction with "more of the same" in their organizational practices. In place of the "old way," leaders are beginning to emphasize new ideas and new approaches to community supervision. This book is meant to illustrate some of those new and important ideas now being invented in the field. Because so much experimentation is going on today, it is not possible to simply summarize the efforts of community supervision leadership to reinvent their field. As you read these selections, however, we call your attention to five themes that emerge repeatedly in the new thinking in community supervision.

1. *Building Partnerships.* Community supervision agencies are tired of being isolated. Too often, when things go wrong (as they will inevitably do when the subject matter is the supervision of offenders), these agencies are weary of having no supporters. And there is a newfound recognition that the complexity of problems faced by offenders and their families is such that no one agency is capable of dealing with the full range of issues required to address offenders who are trying to make it in the community. So, these agencies are starting to form partnerships with other groups. Some of these partnerships are with other government agencies such as police or social services, so that the requirements of community supervision of service and surveillance can be augmented by the efforts of others. Some partnerships are with private sector representatives—foundations, businesses, and natural service partners such as churches. By far, the most significant partnerships are those with ordinary citizens who volunteer their time to help community supervision become more relevant to the needs of the community.

2. *Expanding the Client.* No longer do community supervision agencies see their job as to work only with offenders under conditions of the court or corrections system. Three important new clients have emerged on the scene, and increasingly, community supervision agencies are called on to balance their work with offenders against the interest of these new cli-

ents. The first new client is the victim of crime, and community supervision agencies are now regularly working with victims to make sure they understand how community supervision can be tailored to reflect their interests and concerns about the adjustment of the offender. A second client is the family of the offender under supervision, so that these days, agencies are working with spouses and children to deal with the problems they face as a consequence of their loved ones' involvement in the criminal justice system. The third new client is the community itself, and community needs, interests, and values are increasingly being made a visible and open aspect of community supervision policy.

3. *Focusing on Places.* The concern about communities and victims has given rise to a parallel belief that community supervision must take into account important local differences between "places." That is, different neighborhoods face different problems, and some neighborhoods are homes to large concentrations of offenders under supervision. The idea that community supervision can effectively focus its activity to reflect these important, local differences is a new idea and a promising one. It is an idea that requires officers and agents to leave their "downtown" offices and travel out into the field. It requires the community supervision agency to organize the workload around coherent neighborhoods and enables the community supervision worker to reach out to community leaders and tailor community supervision efforts to embrace neighborhood interests and concerns. And it opens the door for new partnerships with neighborhood groups, service providers, and associations.

4. *Preventing Problems.* Most traditional community supervision is reactive, waiting for problems to happen and using existing policy to decide how to respond to the problems when they come up. The new paradigm is proactive, trying to identify the conditions that create the problems and creating solutions that will keep problems from happening. The expansion of the idea of "the client" to include the victim, the family, and the community serves to broaden the number of interests with which community supervision is concerned and increases the likelihood that small problems can be identified before they explode into large community hazards. By looking at supervision as problem prevention rather than problem reaction, the new community supervision model is actively creative in its style, rather than passively reactive.

5. *Adding Value.* Much of the new community supervision thinking is about adding value to community life. Some offenders are involved in community service that repairs problems in the neighborhood's infrastructure. Others are directly repaying the victim for the costs of their

crimes. Community supervision offices, operating in high-problem neighborhoods, become associated with service provision to people who are not involved in the criminal justice system. Partnerships are used to create new programs that fill gaps in a neighborhood's needs, offering after-school programs, tutoring, child care, healthcare support, and so on. The idea that seems to drive much of this thinking is a concern about the quality of community life, and the new community supervision agency accepts some responsibility for contributing to it. We call this idea "community justice" (Clear and Karp 1999).

Community justice is a new approach to crime that explicitly includes the community in criminal justice processes. It is expressly concerned with improving the quality of community life and the capacity of local communities to prevent crime and to effectively respond to criminal incidents when they occur. A perception of safety, a belief that justice is achieved in response to criminal incidents, and a sense of community among neighborhood residents are the ultimate goals of community justice. Community justice is broadly inclusive of a range of criminal justice initiatives from crime prevention to community policing, adjudication, and corrections. As community justice gains increasing popularity as an approach, it is important to understand not only the practice but also the underlying philosophy (Clear and Karp 1999). The first case study in this book introduces the community justice model, focusing on its four central dimensions: system accessibility, citizen involvement, restorative justice, and offender reintegration (Karp and Clear 2000). We use the example of the Ventura County, California, South Oxnard Challenge Project, a juvenile probation program, to illustrate how these theoretical concepts might work in practice.

Although community justice embraces a number of criminal justice approaches, including community crime prevention (Bennett 1998), community policing (Goldstein 1990; Rosenbaum 1994; Skogan et al. 1999), community defense (Stone 1996), community prosecution (Boland 1998), community courts (Rottman 1996), and restorative justice sanctioning systems (Bazemore 1998; Braithwaite 1999), this book focuses on the crucial arena of probation. Community justice approaches to probation are at the heart of community justice for several reasons.

First, probation is a community-based sentence—it does not involve incarceration. Obviously, the behavior of probationers is of great concern to their neighbors. Second, probation currently has a bad name and is in great need of revitalization. For example, Dennis Maloney, the director of community justice programs in Deschutes County, Oregon (see Chapter 6), describes how he has traveled across the United States talking to community groups, criminal justice researchers, policy makers, and practitioners, yet no one ever praises contemporary probation sentences (Maloney 2000). Never do they say, for example, "He got probation? Good, that will teach him." Most often, people see probation as a second chance (this is good) but do not see it as a strong message to the offender and certainly not as justice for the victim. Third, although many of us have observed the tremendous growth in incarceration in the last two decades—incarceration rates have gone from 320,000 in 1980 to nearly 1.3 million in 1999—we have failed to notice an even larger growth in probation (see Exhibit 0.1). In 1980, the United States had 1.1 million probationers, but in 1999, more than 3.8 million people were serving probationary sentences (Bureau of Justice Statistics 2001). Clearly, a correctional program that places this many offenders in the community ought to be viewed with confidence and hope, rather than the criticism it typically receives. We see community justice approaches to probation as a very promising alternative to traditional probation that might bring back public and policymaker confidence.

Typically, a small domain of concerns conceptualizes criminal justice outcomes. In the contemporary "get tough" era, these are almost exclusively crime control variables: crime rates for areas and recidivism rates for individuals. In former, more liberal times, the domain of outcomes included

Exhibit 0.1. United States Correctional Trends

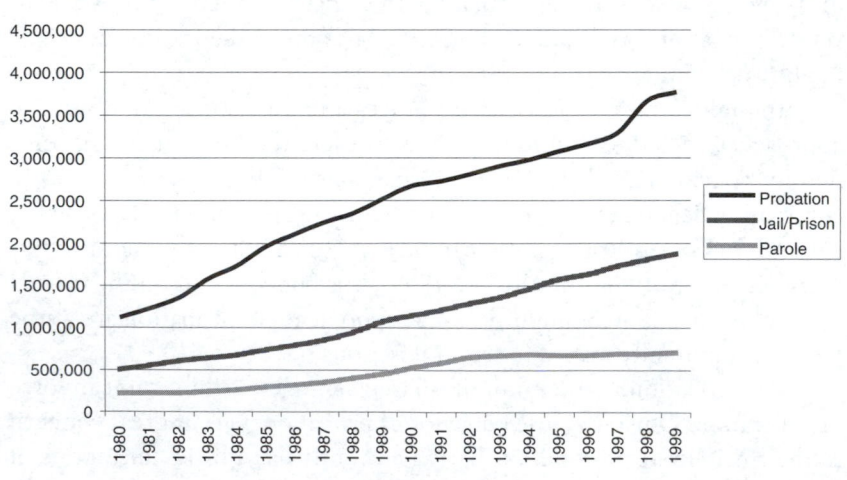

SOURCE: Bureau of Justice Statistics, U.S. Department of Justice.

justice concerns such as race bias in court processing or offender rights protections such as Miranda. They have also included treatment and rehabilitation concerns. This book takes a different approach by conceptualizing justice outcomes from the perspective of community life. This perspective broadens the scope of criminal justice interests without dismissing concerns for individual rights or social order. In particular, community justice emphasizes restoration of the community in response to the damaging consequences of crime and social integration of marginalized individuals, particularly offenders and victims. These twin foci of restoration and reintegration distinguish community justice from traditional probation approaches.

The chapters of this book explore a different probation program in action, each representing the practical side of the community justice ideal. We begin our examination with a new juvenile probation project in Ventura County, California, called the South Oxnard Challenge Project. This case is interesting because it represents a comprehensive vision of the model, although it is still a young program. As we introduce the theoretical concepts behind community justice in this chapter, we explain how the South Oxnard Challenge Project attempts to implement the entire model. The following four case studies (Chapters 2 to 5) exemplify one dimension of the community justice model, allowing the reader to focus on the complexities of each in the context of an existing project. The final case study (Chapter 6) brings all the pieces together, examining a program that is more

Exhibit 0.2. Case Study Locations

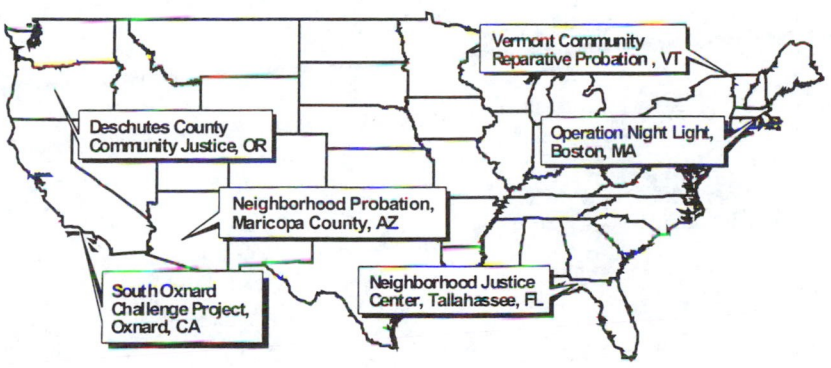

SOURCE: Map reprinted with permission of Alexis Romanow.

mature than the others, more fully implementing the comprehensive vision of community justice (see Exhibit 0.2 for the location of these programs).

References

Bazemore, Gordon. 1998. "Restorative Justice and Earned Redemption." *American Behavioral Scientist* 41:768-813.

Bennett, Susan F. 1998. "Community Organizations and Crime." Pp. 31-46 in *Community Justice: An Emerging Field*, edited by D. R. Karp. Lanham, MD: Rowman and Littlefield.

Boland, Barbara. 1998. "Community Prosecution: Portland's Experience." Pp. 253-78 in *Community Justice: An Emerging Field*, edited by D. R. Karp. Lanham, MD: Rowman and Littlefield.

Braithwaite, John. 1999. "Restorative Justice: Assessing Optimistic and Pessimistic Accounts." Pp. 1-127 in *Crime and Justice: A Review of the Research*, vol. 23, edited by M. Tonry. Chicago: University of Chicago.

Bureau of Justice Statistics. 2001. Washington, DC: U.S. Department of Justice. Retrieved from www.ojp.usdoj.gov/bjs/correct.htm.

Clear, Todd R. and David R. Karp. 1999. *The Community Justice Ideal*. Boulder, CO: Westview.

Goldstein, Herman. 1990. *Problem-Oriented Policing*. New York: McGraw-Hill.

Karp, David R. and Todd R. Clear. 2000. "Community Justice: A Conceptual Framework." Pp. 323-68 in *Criminal Justice 2000*, vol. 2, *Boundaries Changes in Criminal Justice Organizations*. Washington, DC: National Institute of Justice.

Maloney, Dennis. 2000. "The End of Probation and the Beginning of Community Justice." Bend, OR: Deschutes County Juvenile Community Justice.

Rosenbaum, Dennis P., ed. 1994. *The Challenge of Community Policing: Testing the Promises*. Thousand Oaks, CA: Sage.

Rottman, David B. 1996. "Community Courts: Prospects and Limits." *National Institute of Justice Journal* (August):46-51.

Skogan, Wesley G., Susan M. Hartnett, Jill DuBois, Jennifer T. Comey, Marianne Kaiser, and Justine H. Lovig. 1999. *On the Beat: Police and Community Problem Solving*. Boulder, CO: Westview.

Stone, Christopher. 1996. "Community Defense and the Challenge of Community Justice." *National Institute of Justice Journal* (August):41-5.

Our case studies begin with the South Oxnard Challenge Project in Ventura County, California. This is a probation program for juveniles that seeks to implement the broad ideals of community justice. We begin with this case because it is a young program—they are wrestling with the new concept of community justice just as you are being introduced to the concepts here. But they are additionally faced with the challenge of making a new idea work in the real world. As with all new programs, this occurs in fits and starts, and at the end of the chapter, we examine how difficult this can be. Thus, we thought it sensible to begin with a program just getting off the ground as this book was being written and to end our book with a program (Deschutes County Community Justice) that has been around the block, having solved most of its implementation challenges and more fully realizing the community justice ideal. Most important, this chapter not only describes a program in action but also introduces the community justice model, a theoretical framework that guides the organization of this book. The model offers a comprehensive way to understand what community justice is trying to accomplish, focusing on central principles and practical goals. The chapter provides an overview of the model and applies each of its components directly to what program staff are trying to achieve in Ventura County. As you will see, the model has four cornerstones: accessibility, citizen involvement, restoration, and reintegration. The four case studies sandwiched between this chapter and the concluding Deschutes County case each zoom in on one of these four cornerstones. In this way, you will become familiar with the theoretical underpinnings of community justice, but always in the context of a real-world program. One of the themes of the Ventura case study is the idea of place. Community justice has been described as a corrections of place, meaning that we are not simply concerned with individual criminal offenders but also the communities they live in. We do not only ask, Why is the individual misbehaving? but also, What are the social influences or pressures that make people in one community more likely to offend but people in another community less likely to offend? We do not just ask, What kind of person are you? but

What kind of place is this? In this way, community justice focuses its attention on neighborhoods and seeks to develop comprehensive strategies for improving the social environment in which residents live. As such, a key strategy is to develop partnerships between the various service providers within a community. In Ventura, you might find a police officer working with a social worker or a probation officer working with staff of the city recreation department—all of them in search of comprehensive solutions to the myriad problems associated with juvenile delinquency. The challenges of adopting a new philosophy, of implementing a new program, of working collaboratively with community volunteers and multiple community agencies are often daunting. Nevertheless, it is in just such an arena where you find inspired colleagues and committed volunteers. It is a place where criminal justice practitioners become engaged in work they find stressful, to be sure, but also exciting and meaningful. Ventura County is one such place.

Chapter One

Ventura County and the Theory of Community Justice

David R. Karp
Jodi Lane
Susan Turner

On a hot summer day in Oxnard, California, 17-year-old Julio[1] stole a car and committed a hit and run. Julio's childhood was not easy—his mom had abandoned him at birth, and Julio had a history of drug and alcohol problems—but this was the first time he was arrested. On that same summer day, Raymond also was getting into trouble. Ray also came from a troubled family—his dad was in jail and his mom was struggling to make things work for Ray and his four siblings. Ray had begun hanging out with some local taggers, and on a dare, he decided to do some "artwork" on a local alley wall. He too was caught and arrested for the first time. When the police department sent their cases to the probation agency for review, staff there felt both of these young men were at risk for reoffense because they had additional risk factors other than their criminal activity. Consequently, both were given probationary sentences. Yet, probation for each of them meant something quite different. About half of the qualifying youth put on probation received traditional probationary services. Such was the case for Raymond. For him, his responsibilities primarily entailed following his court-ordered probation terms—for example, having contact with his probation officer once a month and attending any services provided by other agencies that the court or probation officer deemed necessary. The other half of South Oxnard youth receiving probation services were assigned to the new, experimental South Oxnard Challenge Project (SOCP). Because Julio was sent to the SOCP, probation meant much more. The SOCP provided a more intensive focus on Julio and his family. In his case, many staff from different agencies worked together as a team to help him and his family improve their daily lives and increase Julio's likelihood of success on probation and afterward. In addition, staff worked with Julio's victim to help him deal with the aftereffects of the crime. Julio's experience represents a new philosophy of probation, a new vision and set of practices that focus equally on the needs of offenders and victims and take advantage of an unfortunate criminal event to improve the quality of community life.

Ventura County: The Context

Ventura County is just north of Los Angeles County on the California coast. Like many coastal counties, the area has a mild climate and is an urban mix of beach and mountain communities. About 750,000 people live there, of which about two-thirds are white and about one-third are Hispanic. The area is relatively wealthy, with only about 10% of the residents below the poverty level, but there are also pockets of poverty (U.S. Bureau of the Census 2000). Oxnard has approximately 70,000 residents and is a primarily working-class, Hispanic community (about 68% of the population) (see Cohen and Associates 1999). Many of the poorer residents live either in the long-established barrio, La Calonia, or in South Oxnard. Because it is one of the highest crime areas of the county, South Oxnard has been a primary concern for police, probation, and other social service agencies in recent years. During the mid-1990s, Oxnard had about 21% of the county's youth population, but the city's youth represented 64% of youth who are incarcerated and 40% of youth on probation, and many of these youth lived in South Oxnard. In the year prior to the initiation of the SOCP, there were 225 gang-related crimes by young people, including 6 homicides and 10 drive-by shootings in South Oxnard (Ventura County Multi-Agency Juvenile Justice Coordinating Council 1997).

In late 1997, the Ventura County Probation Agency received a grant from the State of California to work collaboratively with other service providers to help South Oxnard juvenile probationers. In the summer of 1996, Frank Woodson, then director of the probation agency,[2] read an article by Todd R. Clear that discussed broadening the corrections focus on offenders to also include community members and victims by using community justice approaches to repair the harm from crime (Clear 1996). Woodson was intrigued and brought the idea to the local Multi-Agency Juvenile Justice Coordinating Council (MAJJCC), which was charged with setting juvenile justice priorities for the county. They agreed to use these community justice ideas and request funding from the state for a multiagency, one-stop site for juvenile justice services in South Oxnard. In late 1997, Ventura County was awarded $4.5 million to implement its new program, the SOCP, and the new probation agency director, Calvin C. Remington, his project manager, Carmen Flores, and managers of many other social service agencies set out to implement community justice in South Oxnard.

The SOCP Program and Its Clients

The SOCP uses the community justice approach and has been implemented as a randomized experiment targeting youth aged 12 to 18 years who live in South Oxnard and the bordering community of Port Hueneme. It targets youth who have been cited for a criminal offense or violation of probation and who score at least 12 points on a locally developed risk assessment instrument. On the risk assessment, probation officers score information about the youth's age at first referral, current offense, prior offenses, drug or alcohol use or both, school problems, parental supervision, peer relationships, and out-of-home placements or commitments. Youth with more problems in these areas receive higher scores (up to six points for each problem), making them more likely to qualify for the SOCP. Those who qualify are randomly assigned to either the SOCP, where services are delivered via case management by a multidisciplinary team at a one-stop South Oxnard location (see Exhibit 1.1 for agency participants and their duties), or to traditional probation, where the cases are managed by a probation officer and generally referred out for services.

The SOCP has five broad goals: (1) to develop a more responsive and comprehensive juvenile justice system, (2) to increase youth accountability to victims and the community, (3) to increase family participation, (4) to

Exhibit 1.1. Participants in the South Oxnard Challenge Project

Partner Agencies	Staff Provided On-Site (as of November 2000)	Staff Roles
Ventura County Probation Agency	1 Departmental Manager	Manage project
	1 Part-time Supervising Deputy Probation Officer	Assign cases to staff Supervise project staff
	1 Senior Deputy Probation Officer	Supervise project staff
	4 Deputy Probation Officers	Manage formal and court-ordered informal probation cases; focus on families
	1 Probation Aid	Act as navigator or service coordinator or serve as aid to other staff (depends on skill level)
	2 Office Assistants	Provide clerical support for project staff
Ventura County Behavioral Health Department, Drug and Alcohol Programs	2 Alcohol and Drug Treatment Specialists	Provide individual and group alcohol and drug treatment
Ventura County Behavioral Health Department, Mental Health Services	1 Social Worker 2 Social Work Interns	Provide a modified version of multisystemic therapy for up to 5 clients for 4- to 6-month periods
City Corps (Oxnard)	1 City Corps Program Assistant 3 Work Crew Leaders	Provide community service opportunities (work crews)
City of Oxnard Recreation Department	1 Recreation Supervisor	Provide recreation services and supervise recreation staff, including navigators
	4 Navigators	Facilitate youth use of services
	1 Part-Time Recreation Staff	Lead outings, transport youth, help lead groups
Oxnard Police Department	1 Senior Police Officer	Assist staff in searches, obtaining police reports, and help at day reporting

Exhibit 1.1.   (continued)

Partner Agencies	Staff Provided On-Site (as of November 2000)	Staff Roles
El Concilio De Condado De Ventura	1 Service Coordinator	Provide case management support; focus on families
	1 Community Outreach Worker	Market the project and obtain resources for clients
Interface Children Family Services	1 Restorative Justice Advocate	Provide victim-offender and parent- child mediations
Palmer Drug Abuse Program (PDAP)	1 Counselor	Provide pre-12-step treatment groups for teens

enhance community participation, and (5) to decrease juvenile delinquency. The SOCP usually serves youth and their families for seven to nine months, depending on the seriousness of the case, and, when possible, works with the victim via a restorative justice advocate, who conducts mediations with offenders and their victims or with parents and their children. The community is invited to serve on the advisory board and to become involved in the development and delivery of services. Community youth are also invited to participate in some of the program's activities (see Exhibit 1.2 for community justice-related program activities).

The youth on probation are the impetus for bringing the wider array of services to the offender, family, community, and victim. To give the reader a sense of the youth being served by the SOCP, we briefly describe the characteristics of the 264 youth in the SOCP at or prior to referral.[3] Most youth referred to the SOCP are male (79%), Hispanic (81%), 15 or 16 years old (51%), and live with at least one of their parents (69%, 25% with both biological parents). Most (73%) were referred because of a new citation (arrest) and were on informal probation (67%). Only a third (29%) claimed to be or were suspected by police or probation to be affiliated with a gang or tagging crew. About a quarter of these youth had used alcohol (26%) or drugs (31%) to the point where it interfered with home, school, or peers. Most (68%) had received their first citation by the time they reached 14 years of age. Prior to entry into the program, most youth did not have any prior sustained petitions (only about a third), but those who did were more likely to have been adjudicated delinquent of either property crimes (59%) or violent misdemeanors (19%). There were very few previously sustained petitions (convictions) for violent felonies (8%) or drug offenses (2%).

The Community Justice Model

The community justice model is divided into two domains (see Exhibit 1.3). First, a set of theoretical constructs is summarized by four process-oriented categories: system accessibility, community involvement, reparative process, and reintegrative process. The second domain refers to intended outcomes of the community model, which will be discussed later in this chapter. Because this is a book describing community justice programs in action, it focuses on the "process" of doing community justice. As research on community justice accumulates, we will learn about the effectiveness or the outcomes of community justice, whether or not it really does improve the quality of community life. In this chapter, we describe the left side of Exhibit 1.3, or the process dimensions, in detail by examining how the SOCP has approached the implementation of community justice principles for youth on probation.

System Accessibility

The first process element is system accessibility, which refers to various attempts by criminal justice agencies to make their programs more easily available to the community. Accessibility can be examined based on proximity, flexibility, and informality (see Exhibit 1.4 for measurement indicators).

One way to examine system accessibility is through proximity, which refers to the location of the service center compared to the location of the client base. Services located *within* the served community are more accessible because clients, victims, and community members must not travel far to reach the program, thereby decreasing the time and effort they must expend to participate in the healing process. The SOCP was designed with this specifically in mind. The service center building was located within the heart of the South Oxnard community to help facilitate client access to the service providers and vice versa. Initially, because some staff members had previously been in more traditional units, often located in the city of Ventura, about 15 miles away, they were surprised when they received many unannounced personal visits from the youth and their parents. For example, youth sometimes stopped in after school, and one youth came by every morn-

Exhibit 1.2.   Some Community Justice-Related Activities of SOCP Staff

Staff	Activity
Probation Officers	Increase contact with families of probation clients
	Work with families within their own environments
	Encourage parents to take responsibility for supervising and disciplining children
	Take clients on job searches
	Tutor clients one-on-one in doing homework, studying for tests
	Talk to clients about family and peer relationships
	Facilitate groups
	Work out with clients (e.g., run, play softball and basketball)
	Go on recreation outings with youth (e.g., camping)
	Assist needy parents in obtaining food and furniture
	Talk to neighborhood councils about the SOCP
Child and Family Services Social Worker	Run anger management classes
	Help families clean their houses
	Attend SOCP parenting classes with youth and families
Alcohol and Drug Treatment Specialists	Transport youth to out-of-county activities
	Connect clients to housing and utility services
	Link families to public health services
Mental Health Social Workers	Utilize parent strengths to increase supervision of children
	Teach parents to use praise and encouragement for good behavior
	Assist parents in identifying outside community supports and resources
	Decrease parent reliance on probation for control of their children
City Corps	Conduct community-requested service projects
	Increase youth competency through work and service
	Create an attractive, comfortable environment for youth
Navigators	Be a role model for youth
	Encourage, motivate, and guide youth
	Introduce youth to new life opportunities
	Teach youth skills to navigate life
	Accompany youth on recreation outings (e.g., UCLA football game, camping)
Police Officer	Work with youth on a casual basis (unrelated to offenses)
	Go on recreation excursions with youth
	Take visitors on tours of South Oxnard
	Talk to community residents about the SOCP
Service Coordinators (Nonprobation)	Focus on meeting basic family needs by connecting them with services
	Educate parents about community resources and their responsibilities to initiate the process by asking for help
	Look for existing prosocial activities in community that are congruent with youth interests

(continued)

Exhibit 1.2. Continued

Community Outreach Workers	Recruit community residents for participation in the SOCP
	Obtain community support for and participation in client activities
	Run daily employment preparation groups ("breakfast club")
	Work on local School Attendance Review Boards
	Interact with neighborhood councils and community ministerial groups
	Organize special presentations for and about the SOCP
Restorative Justice Advocate	Connect with victims
	Facilitate healing between offenders and victims, including conducting mediations
	Conduct parent-child mediations

Exhibit 1.3. Community Justice Model

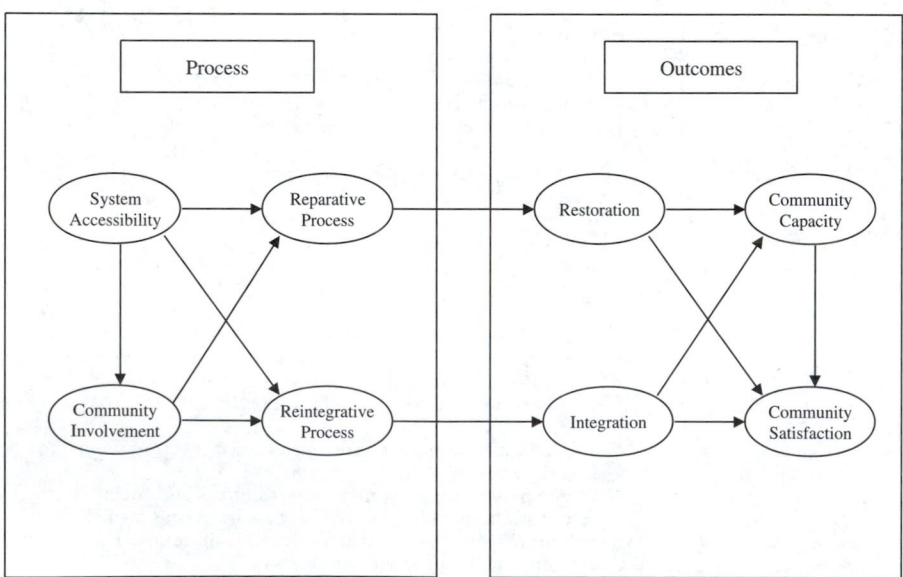

Exhibit 1.4. System Accessibility Indicators

Theoretical Construct	Operational Factors	Relevant Indicators
Location/Proximity	Location of community justice program	Distance of stakeholders to community justice program
Flexibility	"Compartmentalization" of functions; decentralization of staff authority and accountability	Operating hours; range of serivces; rigidity of staff roles
Informality	Responsiveness to emotional needs and other concerns; stakeholder treatment individuals	Rigid and/or adversarial administrative rules/procedures; stakeholders treated personally, respectfully; acknowledgment of rights, dignity

ing for months before going to day reporting or working in the community service program (City Corps Community Service Academy). Although this young man moved out of the area, he continued to stay in contact with SOCP staff, writing them letters and calling to let them know he was okay. Parents also sometimes stopped by to see staff or called to ask for help with their children. Some parents even called to notify the probation officer of "good" things their child has done or to make sure that visiting relatives, for example, will not violate the youth's probation terms. According to SOCP probation officers, parents of youth on traditional caseloads rarely contact them for positive reasons such as these. SOCP probation officers think project youth and their families may feel comfortable initiating positive contacts because SOCP staff spend much of their time out in the community working with youth, their families, and the community rather than conducting office visits and searches like routine probation officers do.

Another criteria with which we can examine system accessibility is through flexibility. When services are delivered in a flexible manner—for example, offering a wide range of services and maintaining adaptable staff roles and nontraditional work hours—programs are better able to administer community justice. The SOCP is specifically designed to offer a wide array of services by staff from different disciplines who work in teams to determine the best approaches to working with each youth and family. The staff have weekly team meetings in which they discuss cases and staff goals for the week. Each staff member takes responsibility for some of the tasks, but their traditional roles often blur as they work together. For example, in the SOCP, probation officers sometimes are leaders who facilitate groups for the youth, even though the groups are sometimes more about family, relationships, and drugs than about probation-related content (e.g., preventing illegal activity). In addition, when clients make phone calls to specific staff members for help, other staff members may be the ones who respond—either due to their immediate availability or because the staff see themselves as working as a team to address youth and family problems. Because staff are given the freedom to be creative in responding to client needs, implementation and program guidelines are fluid. As staff generate new ideas for improving the delivery of services, they are often implemented and maintained if they seem to work. For example, new client groups—such as a Girl's Social Group, Job Club, and Leadership Group—come and go as clients express interest. From the beginning, SOCP managers recognized the importance of having more flexible work hours, because they were aware of research indicating that youth are most likely to commit crime after school on school days and in the early and late evenings on other days (Sickmund, Snyder, and Poe-Yamagata 1997). Consequently, SOCP employees are expected to be available during evenings and weekends. For example, family conferences—meetings where staff work with the youth and family to develop a program plan—are often in the evenings or on the weekends to ensure parent availability. For one family, many staff worked together to help solve crises such as family arguments, sometimes going to the family's home as a team at 8 p.m. or 9 p.m. to help diffuse an immediate conflict situation.

A third criterion of system accessibility is informality, or a release from the formal, authoritarian approach that generally characterizes the justice system. The stereotypical tense environment of the probation office changes to a more comfortable atmosphere in which offenders are included as contributing members in the process. The SOCP has attempted to make its program more inviting to youth, families, victims, and the community so people will come there on their own without being coerced by legal requirements such as terms and conditions of probation. The environment is much different from a typical probation office—there are no metal detectors, bulletproof glass, interview rooms, or probation officers wearing "gear" as part of their daily attire. Although on-site police officers sometimes wear their guns, they are not in uniform, and the probation officers wear their bulletproof vests only when they conduct searches. The remainder of the staff dress in casual street clothes. Because the atmosphere is different from a typical probation office, clients and their families often feel free to walk back into the office area to look for the person they came to see, rather than going to the reception area to request permission to see someone, as they would in a traditional probation office.

Rather than meeting only in interview rooms, staff meet with youth in their offices, outside on benches, or in the community where the youth are located (e.g., in their homes or at school). Some youth have been so attracted to the program that they spent time there daily. For example, for a few months, one youth arrived after school and stayed late into the evening because he did not want to go home. His mother had told staff members that she did not want him as part of the family. Another youth came to see his probation officer every day for awhile to talk about his life and ask advice about his future. Other youth continue to perform community service even after their ordered hours are completed. Some actually initiate projects, for example, asking, "Can we clean my alley today?" Informality also increases the youths' and families' comfort level with staff as many of them come for help unrelated to their probation conditions—for example, social relationships, job opportunities, and homework assignments. Some program youth who attended a five and one-half-month voluntary boot camp program designed for young people having trouble in school chose SOCP staff as their mentors—people to help them transition back into the community upon their release. Others have told their friends about the program, and those youth have then asked for help too. Families have also voluntarily participated in events at the center—for example, making flower arrangements and food, planning and carrying out holiday celebrations, attending Community Advisory Group (CAG) meetings, and mentoring other youth.

Community Involvement

A second major difference between community justice and traditional probation is community involvement in the process. Community involvement can be examined based on the program's ability to identify appropriate people to participate, staff's ability to recruit these people to join reparation efforts, and the level of power-sharing between the enlisted people and the justice administrators (see Exhibit 1.5). Community involvement is grounded in a basic understanding of democratic process—decision making is decentralized, citizenship is valued, residents are invested and empowered (Barber 1984). For the SOCP, there are two general types of relevant communities: the macro community, or the South Oxnard community as a whole, and the micro community, or those who were affected by a specific criminal event (e.g., neighbors, witnesses, victims, or family members of involved parties).

Exhibit 1.5. Community Involvement Indicators

Theoretical Construct	Operational Factors	Relevant Indicators
Definition of sanctioning community	Identification of relevant community and stake-holders	Identification of affected parties by geographic and social indicators
Stakeholder participation	Participation of stakeholders (victims, offenders, etc.)	In/extensiveness of stakeholder participation; recruitment process
Community partnership	Power-sharing by community groups with criminal justice agencies	Nature of agreements between community groups and criminal justice agency; instances of accountability processes

The Macro Community

The SOCP initially focused on gaining support from and addressing the needs of the larger South Oxnard community, in part because groups in this area of the city had long expressed concern that they did not receive needed services from local government. The neighborhood organizations wrote a letter of support for the project, which was included in the grant application to the state. When funding was awarded, local leaders held a community meeting asking for participation and advice about project implementation details, for example, asking what the community wanted most and how they thought it might best be accomplished. Out of this meeting emerged a small group of concerned residents (about 10) who later became the CAG. This group has since merged with the executive board, which initially was comprised primarily of local elected officials and social service organization directors who advised the SOCP on policy matters. The CAG was very energetic and active from the outset, meeting weekly during the program start-up phase and then monthly after that. The CAG initially was concerned primarily about promoting community safety, increasing available services in the community, and ensuring that the grant money was used effectively to address community needs. This group was especially helpful in designating community service projects for program youth such as cleaning alleys, planting flowers or building playgrounds in school yards, and painting house numbers on street curbs. The CAG members also helped with programming by providing entertainment for events, donating goods for project families and recreation services, and giving food to youth who do community service in their neighborhoods. The members of the

CAG expressed an interest in helping community youth and energetically expressed ideas about how the program might best serve the community. For example, one community member suggested the concept of "Challenge U." Her idea was that this symbolic program would be built on the university concept in which youth participate in modules (or classes) that challenge them to become competent young people. SOCP staff did implement a modified version of this idea for youth who were cited (arrested and released) at school. These youth attend three two-hour group sessions in which they are encouraged to look at their behaviors and engage in self-assessment discussions about issues such as relationships, personal needs, self-understanding, and identity. These youth then spend a Saturday doing eight hours of community service and another Saturday doing six hours of recreation activities (e.g., hiking, mountain climbing) monitored by a police officer and SOCP staff. Youth who complete all required activities receive a certificate of completion and have their case closed.

Involving community members beyond the CAG has been a challenge for SOCP staff, but over time, community participation has increased. Community Outreach Workers have been successful in encouraging broader community participation in some typical ways such as food and service donation for clients and their families. For example, around Christmas each year, community members help organize and manage a 20-team, two-day softball tournament in which players are asked to bring toys for project families in lieu of a participation fee. For Christmas 2000, this event collected about 300 toys and gift certificates, so many that the event not only helped fulfill holiday wishes of SOCP clients and families but also provided toys for about 60 second graders in one of South Oxnard's poorest schools. Both citizens and businesses helped sponsor this event. For the 2000 holiday dinner in which SOCP staff and youth prepared decorations and food, a business also donated chafing dishes to ensure that the food remained warm as parents and their children came to enjoy their meal. In addition, community residents helped prepare youth to attend the five-and-one-half-month Grizzly Academy, a voluntary boot camp/education program for high school dropouts sponsored by the California National Guard, which worked with youth on physical training and discipline and helped them get General Education Diplomas (GED). SOCP volunteers helped prepare youth for the Academy beforehand by working on physical training, tutoring, and career development. They also helped organize a barbecue celebration before the youth left for Grizzly. Other community members started out as volunteers and then became paid employees.

The Micro Community

Community justice primarily calls for participation by the micro community: those people most affected by the offense. As useful as the CAG and volunteers are in helping the project with their advice and donations, they cannot substitute for participation by the victim, the neighbors who saw the event, or the offender's family. The SOCP set out to work with two of these groups—the offender's family and the victim. From the outset, the SOCP realized the importance of including the offender's family—both parents and siblings—in attempts to encourage offender accountability and to increase competency in the youth and their family. The SOCP felt this was an especially important component of the program, because juvenile offenders' lives are rooted in their family experience, like all children's are.

After the youth is assigned to the SOCP, the initial meeting with the youth occurs in a family conference. Two or three staff from different disciplines (e.g., probation officer, navigator, mental health counselor, and/or alcohol and drug treatment specialist) introduce themselves, talk to the family about their particular strengths and needs, and sign a Challenge Agreement (and terms and conditions of probation, if necessary). Because many of the youth are not on formal probation, the Challenge Agreement is often adequate and spells out the expectations of the youth and the family, as well as the project staff, in some cases. At a minimum, these conferences include the youth and one parent but also may include siblings and extended family members. Unlike routine juvenile probation, family members have input about the goals of the agreement. For example, parents might want their child to come home earlier, stop using drugs, or stop fighting with them so much. In some cases, staff set up the agreement to work on the issues that the family indicates as a priority for them and listen to parents' input about what might work to help their children. If a sibling of the offender is also on probation, the SOCP probation officer requests the sibling's case be transferred to the officer's caseload, so the SOCP can serve the entire family. If a sibling is not on probation, the parents and sibling(s) are still encouraged to use SOCP services such as a parent support group and recreation events. One recreation event was a camping trip that the SOCP invited families to attend that was sponsored by another community organization but monitored by SOCP staff. Families are also invited to participate in parent-child mediation if there seems to be a lot of anger, fighting, or unresolved issues. If the family has special needs—for example, parental drug use or child abuse and neglect—the staff also work with the family to remedy these issues either by directly giving them services or by referring them to other agencies. For example, in one case where two sisters participated in a mediation after being involved in a fight at school, the mother later voluntarily came to see the mediator to ask for help in a spousal abuse situation. The family eventually worked out the spousal abuse issue on their own by calling the police to have the husband/father removed from the home. The ultimate goal of SOCP service efforts, such as mediation, is to teach the family to be self-sufficient and decrease their dependence on the justice system and other social service personnel to solve problems for them.

Victims comprise another group that has received primary focus from the SOCP. The project has a full-time, on-site restorative justice advocate (mediator), who works to get victims to participate in mediation. These mediators contact victims, often multiple times, to develop a relationship with them and let them know they are available to help them either to get services or just to talk. The mediators also try to show how helpful mediation can be, and although the victims are often resistant at first, many eventually agree to mediation with the offending youth. For example, in one case, a youth tagged a real estate company and etched the building's windows. At first, the owner was resistant and did not want to see the youth or spend more time on the problem, but the mediator talked to her about the power of the youth's facing the victim and accepting responsibility for the offense (e.g., "Remember how you felt when you were little and your mom made you go to someone and apologize to them?"). The owner then agreed to meet with the youth. In another case, in which a young man stole something from a department store, the mediator set up a meeting in the store manager's office, because the manager said the mediator and the youth could have only "five minutes." In this meeting, the manager asked for an apology and "scolded" the boy a bit but then agreed to let him work in the store for eight hours to help pay for his restitution.

The SOCP has yet to systematically incorporate neighbors as participants in repairing harm for particular crimes, but it has been successful in getting offenders to blend with other community members, thereby decreasing the offenders' usual social distance from the remainder of the law-abiding community. For example, youth are encouraged to attend dances sponsored by the local Police Activities League (PAL) to facilitate their socializing with nondelinquent peers. The City Corps group also took youth to Food Share to pack boxes for distribution to needy families throughout the community. At the senior center, which shares an SOCP site, City Corps helped bag and distribute groceries one day a week. In addition, the Girl's Group assisted in a voter registration drive and organized a fund-raiser to help the Tarahumara Indians, who come to the area once a year to raise money for their Mexican village. These youth also served food at the local homeless shelter and helped with gift wrapping at the Salvation Army.

Reparative Process

The third process component is the "reparative process" and is grounded in the problem-solving model common to community policing (Goldstein 1990). Rather than emphasizing strict adherence to precedence and procedure, community justice continually focuses on the problems caused by crime and the problems that cause crime. Where harmful conditions and criminal damage are identified, a decision-making process is undertaken to rectify this harm (Bazemore and Walgrave 1999). Unlike traditional just deserts philosophies, emphasis is not placed on imposing proportional costs on offenders for the harms they have wrought (Clear 1994). Nevertheless, an offender is believed to be in "debt" to both victims and the community. Holding offenders accountable in a manner that facilitates their making amends is a critical part of the community justice process. Traditional punishment that is not directly constructive is outside the community justice model (Bazemore 1996; Bazemore and Umbreit 1995). However, both incapacitation to ensure public safety and potentially onerous work may be requirements of the reparative and the reintegrative processes (which are discussed in the next section).

The reparative process has two components: (1) identifying reparative tasks and (2) ensuring completion of responsibilities (see Exhibit 1.6 for indicators of reparative process). Identifying reparative tasks is often done in a negotiation process that includes offenders and victims. Victims have an important role in specifying how they have been harmed by the criminal incident and what they might need to be "healed." Harm may be identified as (1) material—loss or damage to personal property; (2) personal—ranging from hurt feelings to physical pain; or (3) communal—harm to the whole community's quality of life rather than specifically to the victim's.

One reparative task that has a long tradition in the Ventura County juvenile justice process is restitution, which is the primary means for offenders to repair material harm. In the SOCP, probation officers are expected to prioritize the completion of restitution payments by offenders. For example, when restitution is assigned to a youth, the team often expends great effort to ensure that tasks are completed to help facilitate payment (e.g., a community outreach worker might help the youth get a job, the navigator might take a youth to work every day to ensure the youth can pay restitu-

Exhibit 1.6. Reparative Process

Theoretical Construct	Operational Factors	Relevant Indicators
Reparative decision making	Defining harm and reparation	Identification of reparative needs (victim and community), reparative tasks, and responsibility for repair; nature of reparative agreement
Reparative opportunities	Facilitation of reparative tasks	Reparative service opportunities; staff effort in opportunity building
Victim restoration	Restitution	Receipt of compensation; ratio to losses
	Victim services	Offers for and use of services
Community restoration	Community service	Hours delivered; usefulness of
	Criminogenic problem-solving	Disorder reduction; criminal opportunity reduction; economic development; educational development; family support

tion, and the probation officer might contact the youth on payday to ensure restitution is paid). Sometimes, restitution is not monetary but takes care of the victim's personal needs. For example, one youth painted graffiti on a victim's garage, and his restitution involved painting the garage he had defaced as well as other graffiti that had been painted on neighborhood lampposts by other youth.

In the SOCP, the mediator works with the victim to determine ways to repair the personal harm caused by the youth. The mediator calls victims initially to talk to them about the incident and their feelings about it. The mediator hopes to develop a relationship of trust with the victims so they will feel comfortable talking about feelings, asking for help, and participating in a mediation with the youth. (For an examination of victim-sensitive mediation processes, see Umbreit and Greenwood 2000.) Once the trust is established, the victims often continue to call the mediator, whether or not mediation occurs. Sometimes, it is not until after multiple phone calls or face-to-face contacts that victims feel comfortable identifying some of the things they need (e.g., beyond the monetary restitution usually required by the probation officer) and meeting with the youth. Many victims simply want an apology. Other times, the victims find themselves becoming interested in helping the youth. For example, in one situation, a young man committed a petty theft at a market when he did a beer run and walked out of the store. He was caught, and although the store manager refused mediation, the security guard who caught the boy agreed to participate. When the two met, the boy was embarrassed and apologized with his head down, but the security guard told him it took a lot of courage to apologize, and then offered to go to court on the boy's behalf.

Sometimes, however, victims are not necessarily interested in participating in mediation. Consequently, in community justice projects like the SOCP, staff often work to create reparative opportunities within the community that are relevant to identified needs. One way to judge community justice projects is by the amount of time and energy staff spend doing this. One of the goals is to use the service experience as a learning opportunity. Sometimes the mediator contacts the youth's pastor or another church and asks if the youth can do something for the church as a way to repair harm. As a result, SOCP youth have done many things for local churches such as providing day care for children, cleaning up buildings, and working in reception areas. One youth also worked for her mother's company in the local community doing janitorial work. When opportunities such as these are not available, the youth are referred to programs such as anger management, Al-Anon, and Alateen that fit their needs and might help them become better members of the community.

The SOCP has also gone beyond focusing on individual offenders and now works to improve community way of life as a whole. For example, the Community Outreach Workers organized focus groups where police, probation, and other SOCP staff met with local community members to discuss their concerns—the harm they were experiencing—and to develop solutions to the problems. One of the issues that arose was an increase in graffiti and the community's belief that more gang-related youth were hanging out and committing disorder-related crimes (e.g., vandalism). The community was concerned about these activities being precursors to violence and worked with police and probation to develop solutions to the problems. Some of the strategies included neighbors agreeing to help each other and to call police if they see these disorderly activities occurring and police and probation agreeing to be more visible during the most vulnerable times (e.g., at night) in the most vulnerable places (e.g., hot spots).

Once a reparative need and a solution have been identified by the people involved, carrying out this solution itself requires a lot of effort. Often, solutions require many different staff and agencies to participate, and these staff typically must collaborate to help the offenders and victims complete the tasks. Interagency partnerships and government/community partnerships are often difficult to achieve (Chavis 1998; Grinc 1998; Schorr 1997; Skogan 1996). For example, a probation officer, mediator, and community service organization staff might need to work together to coordinate the supervision and completion of the offender's assigned or agreed-upon duties. Projects like the SOCP are ideally suited for such collaborations, because the staff are all in one building and can work together easily to ensure such activities occur.

Reintegrative Process

The reintegrative process is the final process component involved in defining community justice programs. The goal is to integrate an offender into conventional social life. This primarily means (1) understanding and abiding by the norms of the community, (2) building healthy relationships and strong ties to community institutions, and (3) developing skills and abilities so one can succeed in school, work, and personal relationships (see Exhibit 1.7 for measurement indicators).

Exhibit 1.7. Reparative Process

Theoretical Construct	Operational Factors	Relevant Indicators
Norm affirmation	Articulation of local behavioral standards	Opportunities for norm communication; offender acknowledgment
Offender supervision	Offender risk management	Levels of supervision assessment; risk and protective model; frequency and type of offender monitoring; offender violations of reparative agreements
Support network development	Social ties	Ex/intensiveness of community network
Competency development	Development of conventional competencies for victims and offenders	Array of programs available for competency development; mentoring for competency development, supervision and social support

Norm Affirmation and Offender Supervision

Reintegrative processes begin with *norm affirmation* strategies, which are designed to help offenders conform to community standards of behavior (see also Chapter 3, which describes norm affirmation strategies used by community volunteers in Vermont). It is important at the outset to have clear specifications of behavioral norms to ensure that community justice processes are not used to single out minority groups or individuals who are law abiding but are otherwise nonconformists. Attempts at integration have to balance individual freedom of expression with expectations for conformity. In a society premised on basic freedoms, community justice processes need to be conscientiously specific and justifiable. One approach, advocated by Kelling and Coles (1996), is to hold public meetings where consensus can be developed over appropriate and inappropriate behaviors in public settings. The focus is on problem behaviors rather than types of persons such as homeless people, minorities, or youth, who are often targets of social control activities (Dunier 1999). This approach keeps the focus on controlling *behavior* that clearly harms community life rather than focusing on *people* or *lifestyles* that are nontraditional.

Norm affirmation is a standard activity of traditional probation programs in the setting of terms and conditions of probation that set the standard for the probationer's behavior during the supervision period. Probationers sign these terms and conditions, indicating their agreement to abide by these rules. Offender supervision is closely tied to norm affirmation, as probation officers with routine caseloads monitor these terms and conditions during their monthly office visits and periodic field visits and searches. When rules are not followed, officers may file formal violations of probation, which may result in more rules or incarceration.

In the SOCP, these typical norm affirmation strategies occur, but additional methods are used to ensure youth conformity. During the seven- to nine-month supervision period (depending on the type of probation), SOCP probation officers monitor terms and conditions of probation, ensure youth observance of these rules, and conduct searches, but they also do a broader range of activities. In general, SOCP officers see youth more often and talk to them more about general life activities—for example, their goals, their jobs, their family situations, and the services they need. SOCP officers have noted that both youth and their families seem to respect and trust them more than they did when these same officers worked in the traditional probation unit. This may be in part because officers participate in activities *with* the youth. For example, rather than simply telling a youth to go to alcohol and drug treatment groups, SOCP officers often drive the youth to the group and personally talk to the counselor about the youth's needs. The officers also have taken youth to a job placement office to help them get jobs and taken youth to school.

Other nontraditional activities include physical training and field trips with clients. One probation officer worked out with a group of youth who were going to the voluntary boot camp, and another ran with one of his clients in the morning before work. Officers also go on field trips with their clients—for example, bike rides, museum tours, and university tours—both to monitor clients and to allow the youth to see them outside the authoritarian role, thereby creating what they believe to be better relationships. During these events, officers can spend more time affirming behavioral norms, for example, giving clients ideas about how better to spend their time, how to do well in school, how to avoid negative situations with police and courts, and how to better their lives. Officers have commented that some families do not recognize them as probation officers because their roles are so different from routine probation officer roles. In addition to working with the youth, probation officers and service coordinators work with the youth's family to better their life skills (e.g., teach them how to write resumes and get help from social services). In one case, a probation client's girlfriend became pregnant, and the probation officer chose to work with her to find resources for the baby and to learn how to parent. The hope is that by focusing on the family as a whole, the SOCP will be able to affect youth's environment and better their chances of doing well after the intervention is complete.

In addition to probation officers and service coordinators, the SOCP has many other staff who spend time monitoring youth and providing them with suggestions and help with their lives. All youth receive a navigator, who is primarily responsible for connecting the youth to services and teaching the youth how to navigate these services on their own. Activities include taking the youth to or joining the youth in doctor's appointments, school conferences, etc. In practice, navigators do many other things with youth: running groups, providing friendship, mentoring, guidance, crisis intervention, transportation to and help in court, recreation activities, tutoring, food, clothing, and so on. For some youth, these navigators serve the role of an older brother or sister who gives advice and yet is easy to talk to and "kick it" with. For example, one youth had a problem with other girls in the neighborhood, and instead of responding to their provocation to fight, she went home and called her navigator, who helped her think of another way of coping with the situation. For others, the navigator serves as a substitute parent, who spends most of the time monitoring, giving advice, and sometimes disciplining them—for example, asking them why they are not in school, whether they are using drugs, telling them how to do things differently, and giving them consequences if they do not respond. This navigator role often depends on the needs of the client but also on the navigators' personal styles.

Because the staff work in teams, many other staff also work with each youth, including drug and alcohol treatment specialists, mental health social workers, a restorative justice specialist, community outreach workers, City Corps staff, and recreation staff. These workers provide services based on their disciplinary expertise, but they also provide supervisory roles and promote positive behavior, thereby serving the role of an extended family of service providers. For example, these staff transport youth to and from SOCP activities and other services and visit youth who are institutionalized in the local facilities. They also connect youth and families to services: helping them obtain housing assistance, helping with payment of utilities, jobs, medical care, furniture, and clothing. As they go about their day, each of them also typically talks to some youth or their families or both about their lives and how to make better choices.

Support Network Development

Another important integrative component of community justice programs is helping offenders and victims build support networks outside the justice system (Bazemore, Dooley, and Nissen 2000). This is one way to help youth maintain law-abiding and prosocial behavior in the community. In addition, staff work with youth and families to help them designate other people in their lives who may be able to help them navigate daily life activities. For example, if parents do not have a car, staff ask if there is someone else in the family or a friend who might be able to take the youth to school or to medical visits. Or if youth are unable to make appointments or get to school because they are expected to baby-sit younger siblings, staff problem-solve with families to see if there are other ways of caring for the children. At any one time, approximately six youth and their families receive a modified version of multisystemic therapy (MST) for three to five months. MST is designed to "change the real-world functioning of youth by changing their natural settings— home, school, and neighborhood—in ways that promote prosocial behavior while decreasing antisocial behavior" (Henggeler 1997:2). Unlike traditional mental health services, MST workers are in the field working with youth and families, are available 24 hours a day, 7 days a week, contact the youth and family almost daily, and take responsibility for treatment outcomes, rather than giving responsibility solely to the client. MST will improve youth and family functioning in a way that is maintained over the long term after the social worker leaves the family (Henggeler 1997). Supporters of the SOCP say these intensive services and skills training is one way they can build independence in families.

Competency Development

The third element of reintegrative process is competency development (Bazemore and Umbreit 1995). Youth competency has been the primary focus of the SOCP, because the funding agency is specifically interested in youth outcomes—for example, recidivism, probation completion, and completion of restitution and community service. In addition, most of the staff are primarily trained to work with individual clients (rather than the larger community, for example). Most of SOCP staff time is spent managing cases, monitoring youth, and facilitating services. Each team spends about three to four hours a week discussing its cases and developing the week's casework strategies, and much of the remainder is spent doing actual casework with individual youth and families. Casework is multifaceted and varies, depending on client and family needs. In addition to casework, the SOCP offers some competency-building services on-site, including program components such as City Corps, alcohol and drug treatment groups, 12-step groups, parent support groups, a girls' and a boys' social support group, and open recreation hours.

Obstacles to Successful Implementation

Community justice programs like the SOCP are working hard to change the way probation is designed and implemented in hopes of making the system more humane and more holistic in addressing not only offender needs but also family, victim, and community needs. But probation programs that are working toward implementing community justice ideals often face challenges that make the process difficult. We briefly mention some obstacles here to acknowledge the difficulties faced by probation agencies such as the SOCP, even when there are idealistic and energetic program staff (see Lane and Turner 1999 for a more detailed discussion).

One primary issue probation agencies face is creating and maintaining the program's vision. Because probation is traditionally (or at least recently) law enforcement oriented, many probation officers have been trained to ensure public safety and compliance with court-ordered probation conditions. It is sometimes difficult both emotionally and logistically for officers to break from their training, expertise, and experience to work on what may be perceived in the agency and possibly in the community as "soft" or "warm and fuzzy" (Bazemore and Pranis 1997). They may not know how to "think outside the box"—how to go about delivering services differently. Even if they receive new training, these officers likely will feel more comfortable in their traditional activities. They also may feel they are caught between two conflicting sets of expectations—one from the program, which might ask them to think of alternatives to violating the youth and to help families, victims, and the communities, for example, and another from the agency, which might ask them to focus on public safety, caseload management, and court expectations. Officers may find it difficult to meet both sets of expectations and may choose the safest route for their careers (e.g., promotion)—following the primary agency guidelines.

Collaboration, which is key to many community justice programs, is also very difficult at its best (Chavis 1998; Grinc 1998; Skogan 1996). Agencies and their staff often approach problems from very different perspectives and may disagree about the vision: about the guiding principles, the desired client base, the goals of intervention, and the gauge of success. The same terms (collaboration, teamwork, community justice) might mean different things to different people. For example, programs must ask the following questions: Who pays for what? Are partners equally involved financially? If not, how will the primary agency ensure that tasks are completed? Even if everyone agrees on these things and is equally involved, working together may be difficult in practice—for example, who will do training and what will staff be trained on? Who has primary responsibility for monitoring cases? How and when will client information be shared across agencies? Who makes the final decisions if staff disagree—is it based on consensus, majority vote, or does the probation officer have the final say? What happens if some of the staff do not live up to the expectations of others or complete their tasks? How will the vision be maintained on a daily basis in all the project activities? When agencies work together, issues such as these become magnified, because each agency likely has different ways for dealing with problems when they arise. In addition, when they work together to implement something completely new, such as community justice, the problems are even more inflated. Staff have to struggle with these collaboration issues in the midst of trying to find their way through this new process.

Another issue for community justice programs is defining and involving relevant communities (Karp 1999). Many communities have a group of people involved in community activities (e.g., neighborhood watch, city commissions, and community activism). These folks might be energetic and willing to help (or hinder) the goals of the program, but they cannot substitute for victims and community members who were affected by the crime (e.g., neighbors and witnesses). Including this latter group in the process may be difficult. Victims may not want to participate for many personal reasons (e.g., fear, desire to stay away from the offender, a lack of interest, or a busy schedule), but involving local community members who are affected is also problematic. They may also be too busy or see no benefit in spending time dealing with issues that might seem peripheral to their own lives. But even if the situation is important to them, some people may not feel comfortable participating in justice system activities, especially in minority communities where relationships with officials might be tense or seem difficult to change.

Community Justice Goals: Is it Worth the Effort?

Although often difficult to implement perfectly in practice, community justice programs may be worth the effort, because the traditional justice system has often failed to address neighborhood problems that cause crime and the harm that crime inflicts on communities. Rather than simply focusing on punishing the offender, community justice programs center on the local community as a whole, involve citizens in the justice process, repair the harm of crime, and reintegrate offenders in order to reduce crime, increase justice, and improve the quality of community life. Ultimately, community justice works to strengthen community capacity and increase citizen satisfaction, including their perceptions of safety. The next two sections discuss these ultimate goals.

Community Capacity

Community capacity refers to "the ability to effectively develop, mobilize, and use resources to manage change" (Chavis 1998:85) (see Exhibit 1.8 for measurement indicators). This is consistent with the premise of social disorganization theory that effective communities are able to realize common values (Bursik 1988; Kornhauser 1978; Sampson 1995). Community justice must result not only in just outcomes for offenders and victims but also an increase in a community's ability to solve its own problems. Thus, community justice is a means of achieving *criminal* justice *and* a strategy for community building. Community capacity is reflected in the vitality of local institutions such as families, schools, churches, health and municipal services, and commerce. It is also reflected in the ability of community members to enforce mutually agreed-upon behavioral standards.

Exhibit 1.8. Community Capacity

Theoretical Construct	Operational Factors	Relevant Indicators
Community institutions (families, schools, churches, health and municipal services, commerce)	Socialization Service availability Citizen participation recruitment pool Resource leveraging	Strength of families and schools in the community; community education Creation/expansion of services for competency development, restoration Ex/intensiveness of participation Fund-raising success
Norm enforcement	Informal control in the community	Use of informal control

One indication of community capacity is the extent to which community members are effectively socialized into the culture of the community. In large part, socialization is not a private phenomenon but the work of local institutions and individual community members fulfilling expected institutional roles such as parent or teacher (Bellah et al. 1991). These roles are certainly creatively and variously performed, but their scripts are derived from enduring cultural practices that transcend individuals. When we evaluate community justice programs, we might ask to what extent has the community justice process strengthened these community institutions and facilitated their role in the socialization process? A clearly observable measure is the community's ability to deliver needed services to its members. In community justice, service availability is especially important for competency development (which facilitates reintegration) and restoration, as discussed earlier. Community capacity is also indicated by the citizen participation recruitment pool. For example, is there a roster of volunteers in the community or various networks that facilitate grassroots mobilization? To what extent will volunteers commit their time and energy? Equally important is the capacity of the community to leverage resources for its development. Can it both mount fund-raising campaigns at the local level and garner resources from various sources such as city or state government, foundations, or through coalitions or collaboratives with external partners?

Does the community have the skills, political influence, or technical assistance needed to secure funding for the provision of desired public goods? Community justice programs like the SOCP work to ensure that the answer to these questions is yes.

Community Satisfaction

Community justice also is concerned with citizens' perceptions of the justice system and their experience of community. Although community capacity refers to objective characteristics (what is available), satisfaction is a subjective phenomenon (how people feel). The basic hypothesis is that public sentiment matters and may at times act quite independently of objective indicators, coloring not only public opinion about the justice system but also community identity and attachment (Miethe 1995; Taylor 2001). Community justice is ultimately rooted in the experience of community life, the perception of citizens that their own sacrifices for the sake of the general welfare are reasonably rewarded by the community's provision of public goods (Etzioni 1996). Among the most important returns are three subjective perceptions: a sense of safety, a sense of justice, and a sense of community (see Exhibit 1.9 for measurement indicators).

Exhibit 1.9. Community Satisfaction

Theoretical Construct	Operational Factors	Relevant Indicators
Sense of Safety	Neighborhood fear of crime	Mobility; risk; fear; coping behaviors
Sense of Justice	Remorse/forgiveness	Offender expressions of remorse/ victim expressions of forgiveness
	Offender accountability	Stakeholder views of success in accountability
	Norm affirmation	Expressions of norms; degree of consensus
	Rights protection	Ratio of innocents sanctioned; net-widening
	Legitimacy of criminal justice system	Fairness; responsiveness; capability
Sense of Community	Fulfillment of needs	Perceptions that community meets basic needs
	Membership	Feelings of inclusion, belonging
	Influence	Perceptions of efficacy, making a difference
	Emotional connection	Feelings of commitment, empathy, close personal ties

A *sense of public safety* is a basic component to community life. When people feel unsafe in their community, their attitudes about social life and their resulting behaviors will be affected (Skogan 1990; Wilson and Kelling 1982). Fear of crime is quite common in U.S. society, particularly among women, older persons, minority groups, and urban residents (Miethe 1995). Fear of crime is also negatively associated with community social and psychological ties (Perkins and Taylor 1996). When evaluating community justice programs, we might ask to what extent has a community justice approach reduced fear of crime? To what extent has it increased residents' freedom of mobility through their neighborhood, particularly at night? To what extent do they report fear, competently assess risk of victimization, and alter their behavior in response to crime fears? A community justice approach aims toward citizen satisfaction with the justice system and arriving at a more general *sense of justice* in the community. This is a multidimensional concept. First, is there evidence of a completion in the justice sequence such as expressions of remorse by offenders and forgiveness by victims, or do cases linger without resolution by the stakeholders (Dickey 1998; Gehm 1992)? Second, do community members believe offenders are being held accountable for their crimes (Bazemore and Umbreit 1995)? Third, are citizens satisfied with the normative environment? Do they believe there is consensus on behavioral standards? Do they feel as if they have sufficient opportunity to express their own normative expectations (see Chapter 3 on Vermont reparative boards)? Fourth, do they express concerns over rights protection? Are they worried about the prosecution of innocent individuals, of targeting minorities unfairly, or of an excessive reach by the system? Fifth, do citizens ascribe legitimacy to the justice system? Do they perceive it as fair, effective, and responsive to their concerns (Tyler 1990)? Finally, community justice is a community building enterprise, and the outcomes of this approach should be an increased *sense of community* by its members. On the basis of McMillan and Chavis's (1986) theory, a sense of community is strong when citizens respond favorably to four criteria. First, they believe the community meets its most basic needs—they can find food, clothing, shelter, health care, and so on. Second, they feel a sense of membership or a sense of belonging in the larger social entity. Third, they believe their own contributions to the community make a difference, that they have a sense of influence or efficacy. Fourth, citizens feel an emotional connection to others in the community, bridging their isolation and inspiring their commitment to the community because it is grounded in empathy and personal relationships. To what extent, then, does a community justice process increase these dimensions of community satisfaction? In South Oxnard, for example, we would hope to see South Oxnard residents increasingly satisfied with the justice system and with community life as the project progresses.

Conclusion

This chapter outlines the community justice model and applies it to one probation program. It specifies the critical domains for action and evaluation that distinguish a criminal justice model based on crime control, criminal justice, and community building. This model is grounded in the idea that criminal justice agencies must make themselves accessible to the community and the community must take an active role in the justice process. Foremost, community justice emphasizes strategies that repair damage or solve problems in order to restore communities. Community justice emphasizes strategies that integrate marginal members of the community at risk for further criminal behavior. Ultimately, the success of community justice is predicated on the development of community capacity and community satisfaction. In the next chapter, we venture eastward to examine how another probation program, this one in Phoenix, Arizona, seeks to fulfill the promise of making community justice accessible to the community.

Notes

1. Both Julio and Raymond are fictional examples of South Oxnard juvenile probationers.
2. At this time, the Ventura County Probation Agency was called the Ventura County Corrections Services Agency.
3. We are also studying 275 youth randomly assigned to routine probation, and their characteristics are approximately the same. There are also 41 siblings being followed (30 SOCP youth siblings and 11 control youth siblings).

References

Barber, Benjamin. 1984. *Strong Democracy*. Berkeley: University of California Press.

Bazemore, Gordon. 1996. "Three Paradigms for Juvenile Justice." Pp. 37-68 in *Restorative Justice: International Perspectives*, edited by B. Galaway and J. Hudson. Monsey, NY: Criminal Justice Press.

Bazemore, Gordon and Kay Pranis. 1997. "Hazards Along the Way: Practitioners Should Stay True to the Principles Behind Restorative Justice." *Corrections Today* 59:84-9.

Bazemore, Gordon and Mark Umbreit. 1995. "Rethinking the Sanctioning Function in Juvenile Court: Retributive or Restorative Responses to Youth Crime." *Crime & Delinquency* 41:296-316.

Bazemore, Gordon and Lode Walgrave. 1999. "Restorative Juvenile Justice: In Search of Fundamentals and an Outline for Systemic Reform." Pp. 45-74 in *Restorative Juvenile Justice*, edited by G. Bazemore and L. Walgrave. Monsey, NY: Criminal Justice Press.

Bazemore, Gordon, Mike Dooley, and Laura Nissen. 2000. "Mobilizing Social Support and Building Relationships: Broadening Correctional and Rehabilitative Agendas." *Corrections Management Quarterly* 4:10-21.

Bellah, Robert N., Richard Madsen, William M. Sullivan, Ann Swidler, and Steven M. Tipton. 1991. *The Good Society*. Berkeley: University of California Press.

Bursik, Robert J., Jr. 1988. "Social Disorganization and Theories of Crime and Delinquency: Problems and Prospects." *Criminology* 26:519-51.

Chavis, David. 1998. "Building Community Capacity to Prevent Violence Through Coalitions and Partnerships." Pp. 81-94 in *Community Justice: An Emerging Field*, edited by D. R. Karp. Lanham, MD: Rowman and Littlefield.

Clear, Todd R. 1994. *Harm in American Penology*. Albany: State University of New York Press.

———. 1996. "Toward a 'Corrections of Place': The Challenge of 'Community' in Corrections." *National Institute of Justice Journal* (August): 52-6.

Cohen, Suzie and Associates. 1999. *Ventura County Updated Local Action Plan*. Prepared for the Ventura County Multi-Agency Juvenile Justice Coordinating Council, March.

Dickey, Walter J. 1998. "Forgiveness and Crime: The Possibilities of Restorative Justice." Pp. 106-120 in *Exploring Forgiveness*, edited by R. Enright and J. North. Madison: University of Wisconsin Press.

Dunier, Mitchell. 1999. *Sidewalk*. New York: Farrar, Straus and Giroux.

Etzioni, Amitai. 1996. "The Responsive Community: A Communitarian Perspective." *American Sociological Review* 61:1-11.

Gehm, John R. 1992. "The Function of Forgiveness in the Criminal Justice System." Pp. 541-50 in *Restorative Justice on Trial*, edited by H. Messmer and H.-U. Otto. Netherlands: Kluwer Academic Publishers.

Goldstein, Herman. 1990. *Problem-Oriented Policing*. New York: McGraw-Hill.

Grinc, Randolph M. 1998. "'Angels in Marble': Problems in Stimulating Community Involvement in Community Policing." Pp. 167-202 in *Community Justice: An Emerging Field*, edited by D. R. Karp. Lanham, MD: Rowman and Littlefield.

Henggeler, Scott W. 1997. *Treating Serious Anti-Social Behavior in Youth: The MST Approach*. Washington, DC: Office of Juvenile Justice and Delinquency Prevention.

Karp, David R. 1999. "Community Justice: Six Challenges." *Journal of Community Psychology* 27:751-69.

Kelling, George L. and Catherine M. Coles. 1996. *Fixing Broken Windows*. New York: Free Press.

Kornhauser, Ruth Rosner. 1978. *Social Sources of Delinquency: An Appraisal of Analytic Models*. Chicago: University of Chicago Press.

Lane, Jodi and Susan Turner. 1999. "Interagency Collaboration in Juvenile Justice: Learning from Experience." *Federal Probation* 63/2:33-9.

McMillan, David W. and David M. Chavis. 1986. "Sense of Community: A Definition and Theory." *Journal of Community Psychology* 14:6-23.

Miethe, Terance D. 1995. "Fear and Withdrawal from Urban Life." *The Annals of the American Academy of Political and Social Science* 539:14-27.

Perkins, Douglas D. and Ralph B. Taylor. 1996. "Ecological Assessments of Community Disorder: Their Relationship to Fear of Crime and Theoretical Implications." *American Journal of Community Psychology* 24:63-107.

Sampson, Robert J. 1995. "The Community." Pp. 193-216 in *Crime*, edited by J. Q. Wilson and J. Petersilia. San Francisco: Institute for Contemporary Studies.

Schorr, Lisbeth B. 1997. *Common Purpose: Strengthening Families and Neighborhoods to Rebuild America*. New York: Doubleday.

Sickmund, Melissa, Howard N. Snyder, and Eileen Poe-Yamagata. 1997. *Juvenile Offenders and Victims: 1997 Update on Violence*. Statistics Summary. (OJJDP Publication NCJ 165703). Pittsburgh, PA: National Center for Juvenile Justice.

Skogan, Wesley G. 1990. *Disorder and Decline: Crime and the Spiral of Decay in American Neighborhoods*. New York: Free Press.

———. 1996. "Partnerships for Prevention: Some Obstacles to Police-Community Cooperation." Pp. 225-41 in *Preventing Crime and Disorder: Targeting Strategies and Responsibilities*, edited by T. Bennett. Cambridge, England: University of Cambridge.

Taylor, Ralph B. 2001. *Breaking Away from Broken Windows: Baltimore Neighborhoods and the Nationwide Fight Against Crime, Grime, Fear, and Decline*. Boulder, CO: Westview.

Tyler, Tom R. 1990. *Why People Obey the Law*. New Haven, CT: Yale University Press.

Umbreit, Mark S. and Jean Greenwood. 2000. *Guidelines for Victim-Sensitive Victim-Offender Mediation*. NCJ 176346. Washington, DC: U.S. Department of Justice Office for Victims of Crime.

U.S. Bureau of the Census. 2000. Retrieved October 19, 2000 (www.census.gov).

Ventura County Multi-Agency Juvenile Justice Coordinating Council and Ventura County Corrections Services Agency (MAJJCC). 1997. *Ventura County Juvenile Crime Enforcement and Accountability Challenge Demonstration Grant Application*. Submitted to the California Board of Corrections, March 14.

Wilson, James Q. and George L. Kelling 1982. "Broken Windows." *Atlantic Monthly*, March, 29-38.

The South Oxnard Challenge Project in Ventura County, California, is an excellent point of departure, because it represents a fledgling community justice program with broad vision. We turn now to a probation program in Phoenix, Arizona, that has been up and running for a longer period of time. The Neighborhood Probation Offices in Maricopa County are an excellent example of how probation can become accessible to the community. This case study focuses on how a probation program can realize community justice principles through decentralization, flexibility, and informality.

Making criminal justice programs accessible to the community is the first step in realizing community justice. The simplest way to do this is to establish program offices or officers or both in the community. Obviously, probation services in Maricopa County are located within the county, but in this chapter we deal with probation offices in local neighborhoods. Moreover, the services provided by a local probation office would be directed at those living immediately nearby. The case study focuses on one such neighborhood office, located in the Coronado neighborhood in the city of Phoenix, only two square miles in size and housing only 12,000 of the county's 2 million residents. We focus on this one site to show how programs operate on the ground and how their success largely relies on the kinds of positive social relationships a probation officer can build with a probationer, neighbors, and other service providers such as substance abuse counselors and local police officers.

Local operation of services may seem like a trivial point to dwell on, but such *decentralization* of services is just the opposite of management trends in the last half century. Efficiency usually dictates that services be centralized— that is, why have many small offices when one large office will do? Reading about Coronado's probation offices will provide an answer. For example, we find probationers making more use of the services provided in the local office for the simple reason that they do not have to drive or take a bus to it.

Keeping services *flexible* can also foster accessibility. Each neighborhood, and each probationer, may have a different set of needs. These needs can only be known by having probation officers work closely with the community— probationers, their families, their neighbors—and with other local agencies and organizations so they can learn about local problems and concerns. In Coronado, probation officers work in a satellite office located in a local church building. They work closely with police, often making house calls to probationers together. They worked hard to bring a substance treatment provider to the church building as well. These probation officers do not protect their turf and operate autonomously from others in the community, nor do they simply define their job in terms of supervising probationers. When the community becomes the client, their job description changes—sometimes by the day.

A third dimension of accessibility, in addition to decentralization and flexibility, is *informality*. Coronado probation officers work with law enforcement and have the authority to crack down on probationers for breaking the terms of their probation orders and sending them back to court. And by being active, visible, and widely known in the community, probation officers are a powerful presence. Nevertheless, the relationships they cultivate are based on support and guidance, rather than threat and intimidation. Instead of standing by while probationers complete community service hours, they work side by side with probationers, often on Saturdays, to complete service projects. They also have an open-door policy, rather than keeping visitors to rigid schedules. Probationers and other members of the community often simply stop by, even just to say hello. Perhaps there can be no better measure of successful relationship building than this.

Chapter Two

Neighborhood Probation Offices in Maricopa County, Arizona

Todd R. Clear
Joanna B. Cannon

The Maricopa County Adult Probation Neighborhood offices provide an example of community justice partnerships that span justice agency interests to involve neighborhood residents in crime prevention and community improvement. The Maricopa County community justice initiatives combine a probation mission that balances serving the community and the court with a well-established, community-oriented philosophy in city government that has translated into an interest in neighborhood development. In cooperation with a community-policing philosophy in the city's law enforcement, community justice partnerships have led to innovative public safety programming in five Phoenix neighborhoods. Working closely with residents and businesses in each neighborhood, the probation-based community justice partnerships have resulted in a series of innovative efforts reflective of the needs and interests of these local areas.

This chapter focuses on the nontraditional efforts of the probation department in Phoenix. The ordinary method of probation services—a centralized, office-based supervision of probationers divided into caseloads—has given way to a decentralized, neighborhood focus that accepts as clients the families and neighbors of offenders under probation supervision. This constitutes a subtle shift from probationers' accountability to the court to accountability to the community for the level of public safety and is one of the most significant aspects of community justice in Maricopa County. Instead of a simple focus on the processing of cases, neighborhood probation adds a concern for local capacity to deal with the problems leading to and resulting from crime. The agency thus involves itself in finding tangible ways to improve the community's capacity for "self-regulation" (Bursik and Grasmick 1993) and "collective efficacy" (Sampson and Raudenbush 1999).

The Maricopa County experience illustrates key aspects of the nascent community justice movement. First, the importance of location is illustrated. In Phoenix, we find an example of the way community justice initiatives emerge from an understanding of the unique needs of neighborhoods that are struggling with the problems of crime. Although the probation department emphasized a mission that embraced community safety as a central objective, it is significant that two community justice initiatives described here are efforts in high-need neighborhoods rather than jurisdiction-wide programs. The tendency of the community justice movement is to focus on problem locations rather than legal jurisdictions, and the decision of the Maricopa County probation leadership to begin in these two locations illustrates that approach.

Second, the strategies described here leverage resources to achieve aims of improvement of quality of life in the community and reduction of crime, realizing a connection between the two (Chavis, Lee, and Merchlinsky 1997; Sampson 1995). No new criminal justice funding was used to develop these programs. Rather, the criminal justice agencies reconfigured existing staff and programmatic commitments to concentrate more effectively in these localities. They also mobilized personal resources of offenders and residents to confront problems of disorder that contribute to crime (Kelling 1992; Kelling and Coles 1996; Skogan 1990). Where philanthropic investments had been made in neighborhood action, probation efforts were linked to further leverage resources. The overall strategy shows how community justice may be perceived not as add-on programs to current activities but as strategic rethinking of the allocation of existing resources.

Third, the Maricopa County example shows the centrality of partnerships as the vehicle for community justice activity. The partnerships of the probation department include two-way communication with links to community leaders and other residents and links to state agencies such as police and schools. These partnerships are not only ways to augment services, as is indicated above, but are also ways to change the focus of justice work from individual cases to neighborhood-level problems (Kennedy 1997). Partnerships reduce the chances that cases fall through the cracks, but they also ratchet up the level of concern, from the offender in question to the problems that led to the offending and result from offending. As an extension of these partnerships, informal networks are strengthened toward a greater community capacity. The end aim of partnerships is for the community and representative public agencies to establish common goals and values and to identify available resources, both formal and informal.

The most vibrant example of this community justice approach is provided by the efforts underway in Coronado, a center-city Phoenix neighborhood. Coronado is a neighborhood in transition, with gentrification replacing low-income residential properties and a number of new small businesses emerging to support the demographic changes. Community justice has become an important part of the overall community development effort there. Although each of the five community justice neighborhood projects is unique, they are in different stages of development. In some important respects, the Coronado area most richly illustrates the challenges undertaken by the Maricopa County Adult Probation Department, and so we focus our discussion on Coronado as an illustration of the Maricopa County community justice initiative.

History of the Neighborhood Probation Offices in Coronado

A series of developments within both the Maricopa County Adult Probation Department and neighborhoods in Phoenix set the stage for the advent of neighborhood-based probation offices. The first step occurred in 1995, when the Maricopa County Adult Probation Department decided to revisit and revise its organizational vision and mission statement. The department's effort to articulate a more effective mission is part of a wider effort undertaken in many public service agencies to sharpen the delivery of service by honing activities more closely to a commonly understood mission (Senge 1990). The development of the new mission was an initiative of the department's leadership, but it occurred through a process of agency-wide participation. The mission development activity took almost a year, involved an internal consulting committee, and was finalized through a series of staff retreats. The result was a broadly accepted mission that, among other things, incorporated a greater emphasis on the community. The Maricopa County Adult Probation Department's philosophy is summarized by its vision statement and mission statement in Exhibit 2.1.

In explaining this change in the *Arizona Republic* (Ruelas 1997), Norman Helber, Chief of Adult Probation in Maricopa County, emphasized offender accountability: offenders have "harmed the community, and they're going to pay back that community" by completing community service hours within the community in which they reside and the community in which the offense took place. The mission change in probation created an openness to community initiatives that is atypical of probation departments. For example, Helber emphasized the importance of neighborhood specificity by assigning officers to supervise probationers in particular communities. In fact, during the very beginning stages of the Coronado Neighborhood Probation Office, probation officers staffed at the neighborhood office found themselves with slightly smaller caseloads than probation officers at the central office. In turn, these Coronado probation officers were given additional cases outside the Coronado neighborhood. This, however, caused increased paperwork, and caseloads skyrocketed, thus becoming more like traditional probation practices, which damaged the neighborhood level effort. In an interview with Leslie Ebratt,[1] Coronado Probation Supervisor, Ebratt explained that Helber "didn't like that and his direction was to go back to pure Coronado," allowing for the importance of and potential for community specificity to be recognized.

The changes in the Maricopa County Probation Department mission can be seen, in part, as a product of shifting policy emphases in the areas served by the department. Phoenix, the largest city in the county and the one contributing the greatest share of probationers, is a forerunner in an increasing national trend toward "community development" or "community empowerment." The *Phoenix Downtown* magazine quotes Kate Wells, Coronado resident, as saying, "From everything I have reviewed regarding other communities across the country, Phoenix is way ahead in departmental design and delivery of services to neighborhoods from the police department to all aspects of the Neighborhood Services Department" (Johnson and Ashley 1997).

As previously described, the Coronado neighborhood in center-city Phoenix had been experiencing decay and rising crime rates. A 1990s' resurgence in this area of Phoenix occurred in part because the neighborhood is convenient to these residents' places of employment. A strong voice from

Exhibit 2.1. Philosophy of the Maricopa County Adult Probation Department

---

Vision Statement

An agency of professionals committed to continuous improvement in the quality of community life by offering hope to neighborhoods, victims, and offenders.

Mission Statement

To enhance the safety and well being of our neighborhoods. We accomplish this by:

Working in partnerships with the community to provide prevention and intervention services;

Providing reports and significant information to the courts;

Managing offender risk by enforcing court orders, affording opportunities for change, and expecting positive and law-abiding behavior;

Facilitating victim involvement and restorative justice services;

Recognizing and rewarding staff performance and achievement;

Promoting excellence in service and innovation in leadership.

Values

We Believe:

People can change and that probation services are the most viable means to effect positive change;

In treating all people with dignity and respect;

In promoting and maintaining a positive, safe, and healthy work environment;

In shared leadership with staff and community;

Staff are the greatest resource in accomplishing our mission.

---

residents in Coronado expressed a desire to improve the quality of life in the community—where a special emphasis of this concern was crime.

The pursuit of improved neighborhood life is one of the reasons that one Coronado citizen says a group of residents, acting together in the mid-1990s, decided to "aggressively pursue grants" to revitalize their community. They were successful. In 1996, Coronado residents were awarded a Heritage grant for historic preservation, a type of funding previously only available to full-fledged cities, not neighborhoods. The Coronado neighborhood won an approximately $800,000 grant, gaining considerable acclaim. Soon after, the police department, and in particular the community action police in Coronado, approached the Coronado neighborhood association to jointly apply for a Comprehensive Communities Program (CCP) grant, which they were ultimately awarded as well. A citizen stressed that one reason why this community was so successful in receiving grant money was that an active community member worked for the city and knew the appropriate contacts and procedures necessary to apply for these grants. Having a community resident with the knowledge of these processes gave Coronado an in.

After the CCP grant was awarded, Coronado residents polled the various local agencies to determine how they could use the grant money to alleviate citizens' concerns about their neighborhood. Juvenile delinquency was reported to be a concern, so residents went to the juvenile probation department and asked what they could do about delinquency with the assistance of the residents. A pilot community juvenile court resulted. A juvenile community justice committee comprised of trained citizens facilitated dialogue between citizens (who were often the victims), juvenile offenders, and the parents of the juvenile offenders. Each party influenced the sentence of the juvenile offender. Since Coronado began this juvenile program, 25 others have begun in Maricopa County. The community group also began educational classes such as General Education Diploma (GED) training and English as a Second Language (ESL) classes, which had been identified as important to the community.

Soon after these initial innovations, the Coronado residents met with Adult Probation staff who were proposing the establishment of a satellite adult probation office in the Coronado neighborhood. Coronado identified office space in a neighborhood church for the probation officers to work out of, and the probation department assigned staff to the office. Staff volunteers selected for assignment to this office were those deemed to possess good people skills and an interest in a more community-oriented focus to probation, including flexibility and creativity in the way they supervise offenders.

Thus, the Coronado community justice initiatives stem from community activists interested in problems of crime and justice. The desire among Coronado residents to organize evolved into a series of grants and a small group of active, motivated Coronado citizens dedicated to improving local governmental services. The work of these residents spawned a willingness on the part of local agencies such as the police and probation departments to innovate and led to a series of community justice initiatives.

Since the Coronado office opened, other neighborhood probation branches have been developed in five Phoenix neighborhoods. These programs have been allowed to develop along their own paths. The differences underscore the way community justice enables the development of a variety of neighborhood-relevant programs, the composition of which differs from one local area to another. What makes the array of programs appropriate is not that some other area of the city has them, but that they are needed in the particular area of the city where they have been developed and operate. The nature of the community—in particular, the problems of crime and safety in that community—are the forces that drive the design of programs, not external programmatic objectives.

The Coronado Community

The Coronado neighborhood comprises about two square miles and houses some 12,000 residents. The neighborhood is comprised primarily of occupant-owned, single-family homes, with a smaller representation of rental homes and apartments. There are distinct demographic differences, block by block, including disparities in income levels from one area to another within the community. Hispanics constitute a slight plurality among ethnicity groups, but English-speaking residents outnumber Spanish-speaking residents overall. The majority of the residents age 25 and over have a high school degree, and many have some college experience.

Coronado is not a wealthy community: most households report an annual income under $30,000. Although a substantial amount of money for revitalization came into Coronado, some areas of the neighborhood seem to be experiencing decline. As mentioned, Coronado is an inner-city community that had been experiencing increasing crime rates and deterioration. For example, prostitution has been displaced into one segment of Coronado as a result of stings in the nearby Garfield neighborhood.

A core group of Coronado residents were activists about revitalizing their neighborhood through efforts such as pursuing the CCP grant and contributing time and their own funds to work with agencies and to promote active neighborhood associations, and these citizens were vital for community justice in their neighborhood. But the citizen initiative is only part of the story. The vice president of the Greater Coronado Neighborhood Association partially attributes his involvement in the neighborhood association to a probation officer. He tells of how he had long-standing concerns about a house on his street that seemed to have a lot of drug activity. He complained to fellow residents at a neighborhood association meeting that the association "didn't do anything." The community probation officer in Coronado responded to him by asking what he was doing. He says this made him look at the situation differently, seeing a need for a collective and constructive approach, and then became an involved resident in community action.

Maricopa County may be seen as displaying three elements of readiness for community justice: (1) a philosophy of government that embraces community development as a public value and expresses priority in justice agency objectives that emphasize community-level concerns, (2) a core group of active residents within a target community who seek to organize and confront public safety problems, and (3) an identifiable pool of resources that may be targeted to advance community justice initiatives.

Philosophy of the Coronado Neighborhood Probation Office

The philosophy of the Coronado Neighborhood Probation Office is to collaborate with local agencies to assist the members of the Coronado neighborhood in creating a safer community and, ultimately, a better quality of life, using citizen input and participation as the central technique. One officer points out that the role of the probation office is to facilitate citizen action toward an improved sense of security by becoming a resource for citizens. The probation office promotes three key concepts:

1. Awareness in the community,

2. Partnerships in the community, and

3. The exchange of knowledge and ideas among community members and influential parties to create innovative techniques to guide offender supervision and community development.

Although no formal surveys have been conducted to determine the community issues that are most problematic to citizens and to ascertain the types of solutions citizens would propose for these problems, effort has been made to garner this information. Informally, surveys were conducted through the neighborhood association about what types of resources were available in the community and what types of issues were of concern to Coronado citizens. At neighborhood association meetings and in the neighborhood probation office, communication about these issues occurs between staff from the probation department, other government agencies, and residents.

When they established this office, probation officers made it a priority, in a series of community meetings and small-group conversations, to discuss citizen concerns about locating a probation office in their community.

Residents expressed the concern that additional offenders would be brought into their community with the location of a probation office in their neighborhood. However, the plan called for the office to deal exclusively with probationers living in Coronado, so that probation officers in the neighborhood office would simply be able to more closely supervise probationers who already were or would be residing in the community. Probation officers also suggested that the community could anticipate more productive use of probation officers' services by residents under community supervision. For instance, officers would be able to stop in on probationers more frequently and without notice, increasing the quality of information about probationers' activities. In the same vein, probation officers would easily be able to speak with family members, neighbors, and employers of probationers.

The images of improved supervision and surveillance helped to sell the community on the value of a community office, but these should not be seen as the central motives for probation efforts in that office. A Coronado probation officer describes the neighborhood program's philosophy as *not* telling people what the probation department can do for them but instead asking what people would like the probation department to help citizens accomplish in their community. The emphasis on improved supervision came in response to the interests of the community members in having a local office. This type of responsiveness helps build community confidence in probation practices.

Maricopa County Adult Probation supervises offenders in the community while using methods that reflect residents' community development aspirations. The importance of the community connection is illustrated by a discussion of some of the central aspects of the work carried out in the office.

The Coronado Probation Office

A single probation unit serves the Coronado area. Three probation officers work there on a daily basis with one supervising officer who works from the downtown, central Maricopa County Adult Probation Office. These three probation officers supervise approximately 235 English- and Spanish-speaking probationers residing in Coronado. The probation officers work solely with people living in Coronado (with the exception of one officer who, because of his fluency in Spanish, supervises some Spanish-speaking probationers in the adjacent Garfield neighborhood).

The office is located in donated space at the back of the Covenant Presbyterian Church in Coronado, which is often referred to as a community center. The church building has earned the name community center because other community services are offered through this church, including a satellite office for Maricopa County Juvenile Probation, Modest Means Legal Services, and Betania Adult Education Center, which provides GED and ESL classes, and job placement and training, as were requested by residents. According to one officer, recently the probation officers met with and sought the favors of a local counseling center to begin offering services out of the church with sliding scale fees. This local mental health service is not simply offered to probationers but is available to all community members, making affordable counseling within walking distance of most residents. Also housed at this community center are playground equipment for citizens, arts and crafts, and a tool shed. The shed is described as something that has been in demand and well used by probationers and citizens alike, particularly during times when probationers have helped make repairs to the church.

The importance of providing local probation offices with an array of services is worth emphasizing. It enables probation officers to have more effective contact with social services, making them aware of concerns expressed by community members to staff of these services and helping shape their effectiveness with Coronado's probationers.

Coronado probation officers have slightly larger caseloads than most Maricopa County Adult Probation officers. But the caseload numbers are somewhat misleading. In a sense, community justice defines the entire community as the caseload, because accountability of the neighborhood probation department is to the community. Thus, a community probation officer's caseload includes the probationer, the probationer's family, the probationer's neighbors, and, in fact, the community in which the probationer lives. This change cannot be accomplished without reconsidering multiple aspects of traditional probation work from the mission statement of the agency and the job description of the probation officer.

In traditional probation practice, work with a probationer caseload is defined in terms of a specified number of "contacts." Obviously, under a community probation model, probation officers cannot meet with each citizen in the community. The probation office can make a systematic effort to incorporate the community into the probation agenda. Opportunities can be made available for all citizens in a community to be active and influential in the regulation of the community. Community-specific probation offices charge their staff with becoming familiar with the resources, networks, and dynamics of particular communities, and they can use those resources to strengthen their work with probationers while tailoring efforts to reflect broader community interests. This has been the challenge of the Coronado office.

The open-door policy maintained by the probation office allows for probationers, community residents, police, and so on, to easily visit the office and discuss community issues. For example, sometimes a probationer stops in to pay restitution and other times simply to talk. One probationer said, "I come by to visit every once in awhile; we clown around." Frequent, unplanned visits to the office are common not only from probationers but from residents, police, and others. This has fostered partnerships that build relationships and share information between probation officers, probationers, community members, and personnel from other agencies such as the police.

Although the frequent, informal visits of nonprobationers may be understandable, the visits from probationers did not exist when the probation officers were located in the downtown office. Probation officers speculate about this pattern of informal visits: the probationer happens to be walking or driving by, or the probationer recently completed some community service around the church and this work has fostered a sense of belonging and a sense of comfort with the probation office environment. Perhaps probationers find the neighborhood location useful because it eliminates the need for them to locate transportation to or take time off from work to report to their probation officer at a downtown office.

Ebratt tells how while working with probationers doing community service one Saturday, she asked them how they felt about the new neighborhood office. One probationer responded that he felt like his probation officer cared more about him, his family, and his work. The probationer also said that he stops in the office because it is easy to do so. Another probationer responded that the new office was "homier." These perceptions may be attributed to the officers being more accessible, making more house calls, meeting the probationer's family and neighbors, and realizing each probationer's particular circumstances. These changes foster a sense of comfort on the part of the probationer. In combination with more frequent, unplanned meetings, they may make the office seem less alien and formidable to clients. Each of these changes is made possible by locating an office within a particular neighborhood.

Community probation officers have also begun to develop innovative, informal techniques of supervision. In a typical example, Ebratt tells of a probationer, "Marty," who was suspected of violating the terms of his probation. Some of Marty's neighbors suspected that he was using and selling drugs again and perhaps had been involved in burglary. These neighbors informed both police and probation about this concern, though nothing was proven. Ebratt then suggested setting up an intervention to include Marty, probation staff, Marty's family members, and one or more neighborhood residents. This intervention was not intended to result in Marty's arrest but instead to prevent his arrest by allowing him to know that the police and probation were informed of his possible violations and also that citizens and probation staff cared enough about him to try to intervene before official action took over. A community member said, "We would think he has the ability to turn it around and get back on track. We just would want him to know that we are watching without being confrontational or threatening." The linkages to community members and the availability of residential supports to probation efforts make this kind of intervention possible and give it the chance to succeed.

Probationers frequently stop by the office because it is located in the neighborhood. Therefore, the office serves as a reminder that probation officers could be monitoring probationers at any time and driving by probationers' homes or workplaces. As a probationer stated, this gives a lot of "power" to officers, although this power is not necessarily perceived as authoritarian. This power is more accurately seen as emanating from the location of the office and is a product of the fact that officers are extremely visible.

Building Community Justice Action

During the past two years in which the Coronado neighborhood office has been operational, the benefits of this neighborhood location have been apparent to probation officers, probationers, and residents, and all have benefited from the office. Probation officers say they are able to more closely supervise probationers, probationers feel the presence of officers more significantly, and the accessibility of the office enables increased communication between officers, citizens, and probationers. But efficiency in supervision is not the main objective of a community justice approach. The aim of the community probation office is also to become a presence in the community, to show how the probation office accepts a responsibility to improve the quality of community life.

Community justice asserts that meaningful justice is best accomplished at the community level. Differences in community life require that justice action be community specific, reflecting differences in local characteristics, resources, and dynamics. To determine what the probation department's role would be in achieving community justice, Maricopa County Adult

Probation addressed a series of policy questions raised by a move to community justice:

- Why is it important to consider, and what are the benefits of considering, the probation department as accountable to an entire community, rather than just probationers?

- How can the location of a neighborhood office facilitate the integration of the probation department into other networks in the community so the probation department would be considered a resource for the community?

- How can the location of an office in the neighborhood increase supervision of probationers and, thus, increase public safety?

- How can it be ensured that most citizens and factions in the community reap the rewards of these benefits?

After the administrators of Maricopa County Adult Probation decided to establish neighborhood offices, they turned to the task of clarifying the role citizens would play in their neighborhood probation service. Flexibility and informality in program structure and operations were necessary to enable administration and probation officers to tailor their functioning to reflect the concerns of Coronado citizens. Traditional centralized or standardized design would have restricted the program's ability to adjust to particular community needs. Therefore, steps were taken to discern what Coronado residents wanted to see happen in their community and what role a neighborhood probation office might play in achieving these goals.

The development of a community probation office leads naturally to a series of questions, among them: Do citizens want a community probation office? What role do citizens think a neighborhood probation office can play, and what role are citizens and other parties in a neighborhood willing to play in guiding the probation department? What resources and dynamics do citizens feel are important for community development? Thus, one of the first steps was to gain an understanding of how Coronado's residents felt about locating a probation office in their community.

Informal methods of obtaining information from citizens were used. Probation officers attended neighborhood meetings, met with police patrolling the area, and simply asked citizens from the community what the citizens thought the community needed that a neighborhood adult probation office might be able to assist with. In addition, probation officers volunteered to work on community projects, and as mentioned, probation officers worked with probationers on Saturdays while probationers performed community service hours in the neighborhood. By taking these proactive initiatives, officers gained the respect of the citizens. In addition, citizens witnessed, from the beginning and as an ongoing occurrence, officers soliciting citizen input and spending time in the community. These activities "allowed people to get involved by chance and then find out that it's not that uncomfortable [to work with probationers and the criminal justice system]," a resident said.

Coronado probation officers used flexible schedules (as explained, weekend hours are often part of the job) with probationers doing community service in the neighborhood. The types of community service have included repair to the church roof where the office is located, repair of one resident's yard and porch, and the painting of a mural on a graffiti-covered wall. One community member has proposed that the probationers could do community service by distributing neighborhood association meeting flyers door to door in the community. He said, "In that way, they [the probationers] could go door to door and meet people on a first-hand basis and talk to a lot of people and get to have a different perspective." The lesson has to do with concerns on the part of Coronado citizens for public safety and the perception of probationers by citizens in the community. Probation officers supervise probationers doing community service, and Coronado citizens have come to trust the judgment of the probation staff in determining who the appropriate candidates are for different types of community service. According to Ebratt, it is the probation office's policy not to allow violent offenders to do certain types of community service that would put them in close contact with citizens and citizens' residences. Indeed, a resident said that, at first, citizens were leery of having probationers do community service so close by. However, now he says he feels most citizens "have gotten used to it," and no negative incidents have occurred to increase citizens' fear. Another citizens' attitude illustrates this shift in public perception. She said she helped probationers do community service repairing the local church, which also houses the neighborhood probation office, one Saturday, "while I was eight months pregnant, and I did not feel afraid at all."

Probation officers attend weekend and evening neighborhood association meetings and activities. This keeps probation staff current on issues in the neighborhood and active within neighborhood projects. For example, in October 1998, officers were attending a Crime Summit meeting initiated by the Coronado Neighborhood Association president and open to all Coronado residents. At this meeting, a Phoenix Police Department detective spoke about the development of community courts in the neighborhood.

The openness to community concerns paid off in improved interactions between probation professionals and residents of Coronado. Citizens ask the probation department for assistance with community projects and improvements for which probationers can receive credit for community service hours. A resident says that currently citizens are reporting a realization that by allowing probationers to do various types of work in the community, the community is strengthened, which ultimately benefits everyone, including residents, business owners, and probationers.

The variety of efforts to incorporate community justice into the mainstream of community life has not been lost on residents. As a citizen stated:

> We feel like these people [probation staff] live here, in this neighborhood, because they invest a lot, even after hours, I believe, into this neighborhood and they know this neighborhood better than even some of us do and that kind of motivates us to be involved. I mean the more that we feel people really care about us, the more we want to get involved and we feel like we are not really wasting our time.

Expanding the Boundaries of Probation Activity

Traditional probation operates as something of an isolated justice function, lacking connection to communities and other justice agencies. Probation workers sometimes enjoy close relationships with the courts (which also tend to be isolated from the community), but otherwise most of the relationships formed by probation activity have an informal, fleeting quality. The lack of systematic relationships helps to make probation vulnerable to the ebbs and flows of its critical environment. A justice function without friends, probation often appears to be a justice function without champions.

The community justice version of probation actively seeks to form partnerships in order to pursue community justice aims. Partnerships require time and attention for probation staff, shifting resources away from supervision of clients toward developing strategic collaborations. The belief is that these partnerships, effectively built and sustained, will contribute to a significant improvement in the way a stronger community presence indirectly increases the quality of supervision and services for probationers.

The Coronado office actively pursues three types of partners for its community probation activities. A primary partner is the police department, which is a natural ally due to its well-established community-oriented policing philosophy. A similar partnership is formed with service delivery agencies in Coronado that are primary sources of support for probationers. Probation also actively seeks citizen partners: Coronado residents and businesses that want to volunteer time and resources to contribute to a stronger community.

Police-probation partnerships have become popular in numerous locations across the United States. In Phoenix, both the police and probation staff have recognized the importance of establishing this partnership. Probation staff relied on the police unit in Coronado when they first attempted to establish the probation department in the community. The first steps were simple. Probation attended the popular, regular community meetings involving the police and residents to help build trust between the community and the probation department, and by having police accompany probation officers on visits to probationers' homes, a public sense of shared interests between the two agencies was developed. This created a situation in which police, probation staff, and probationers meet each other under informal circumstances, allowing for the breakdown of barriers or an "us against them" attitude, which has often dominated the three-way relationships between police, probationers, and probation staff.

A natural product of this partnership is a formal and informal pattern of information sharing. The creation of a common information base reduces the community isolation of probation as well as the antagonism between police and probationers and sets the stage for a shift in the long-standing adversarial quality of relations between residents and justice agencies. Probation officers share information with police officers about who is on probation so that the police can assist the probation department in supervising probationers. But this altered role with probationers can reorient police attitudes from a tradition of suspicion and hostility to a potential for responsive support. One resident describes it as "a little information network; it's very casual." In place of opposing relations, a new norm of problem solving within the community is promoted.

A more formal version of partnership is accomplished through activities such as Block Watch, which is a type of neighborhood crime watch program. Block Watch meetings are held once a month and are attended by citizens, probation officers, and police officers. Information is shared, and citizens notify probation officers and police officers of suspicious activities, sometimes regarding probationers. Approximately 45 active block watches exist in the Coronado neighborhood, according to a resident. Citizens are actually trained and educated about Block Watch from the police, and this contact fosters relations between the groups, making citizens feel more comfortable about communicating with the probation officers and the police.

Probation officers work with job developers in the community to identify employment opportunities and job training for probationers and give probationers information about who to contact for these jobs. This assistance is different from traditional probation, because when done at the neighborhood level, officers can give specific contact information to the probationer and perhaps even call the potential employer with the probationer present. Access is increased, and officers can expect that probationers will contact potential employers shortly thereafter. Thus, probationers have no excuse not to pursue these opportunities, which is different from traditional probation and increases accountability. As Ebratt explained,

> They [probation officers] have a one-on-one relationship with people in the community, which makes all the difference in the world. It is so different than giving someone a number and saying by the time I see you next month you need to call this person across town and do this, that, and the other, and you can tell me about it in thirty days. Well, once they leave the office, it is not going to get done.

Private citizens also become a type of partner in the way they provide information about community activities. Probation officers gain a great deal of information from residents who just stop by the office to talk and from attending community functions, but officers have also solicited community assistance with certain projects. Citizens help determine ways probationers can do community service that will benefit the community, and they also provide direct support for supervision. Officers are generally selective when deciding which citizens to ask for help because of privacy concerns. However, certain cases present public safety concerns or are severe enough to warrant asking for assistance from community members. One such case involved domestic violence.

A probationer who had been arrested for domestic violence began living with his wife, the victim, again. Offenses continued and, in fact, were thought to be escalating to the point that the victim's life was in danger. The latest offense involved the probationer holding a gun to his wife's head. Probation staff went to a neighbor, who was also the victim's mother, introduced themselves, and expressed an interest in trying to keep the victim safe, not necessarily in arresting the offender. Staff provided the victim's mother with information on how to get in touch with probation officers if she saw any alarming activity. Staff also requested police assistance in supervising this offender. Probation asked that if the police were called to the house for any reason, probation staff be notified. Therefore, probation is working in conjunction with private citizens and other agencies such as law enforcement.

Maricopa County Community Probation: Lessons and Concerns

The Maricopa County Adult Probation Neighborhood Office (and the other neighborhood probation programs in Phoenix) illustrates several important aspects of the community justice movement. By selecting distinct neighborhoods and reorienting resources toward them, the potential for innovative services in concentrated local doses is demonstrated. By leveraging resources through philanthropic investment and agency partnerships, the community justice model has shown how the concept need not be seen as a "new program" but rather as a strategic way of using existing resources to target problem locations. Partnerships also increase the integration of probation functions with other aspects of community life.

Location, innovation, and partnerships are community justice components that are illustrated by the Coronado project and demonstrate how a probation agency can embrace community justice orientations to the mutual advantage of the community, the probationers, and the agency. But not surprisingly, each of these potential advantages of the community justice orientation raises issues for the probation function. Below we discuss the way in which the move toward community justice in Maricopa County has uncovered managerial and policy issues that have to be addressed in the community justice agenda.

Going Local

A Coronado resident captured well the paradoxical concept of a local probation office and community justice:

> If it's really truly going to be community-based, it is going to be different every single time based on the needs of every community [but] it can be duplicated.

In theory, each office is different, because each community is different. And although the Coronado office is in some respects the most well-established neighborhood probation office in Phoenix, other offices also have programs underway—and the differences between the neighborhoods and their probation offices are becoming apparent. This raises two distinct but related problems: consistency in services and competition in services.

The central question of consistency in services is this: To what degree may two communities within the same legal jurisdiction differ in the types of services they offer to residents? Of course, some flexibility in services is always present, because Phoenix and Tucson are both big cities under the same Arizona penal code, yet they have distinct differences in probation practice operated under different agencies. But when these differences occur in adjacent neighborhoods served by the same agency, then profound questions of equal protection are raised.

Differences in neighborhoods include differences in ethos and culture. To what extent may these differences translate into legal practice? At this point, we have no examples from Phoenix to illustrate this problem, but it is easy to imagine one neighborhood in which residents become so concerned about truancy that at-risk juveniles there start to be treated differently from juveniles in other neighborhoods. There is already a juvenile community court in Coronado—does this focus benefit the neighborhood's juveniles or disadvantage them, compared to other areas of Phoenix? How much different treatment, and of what kind, is acceptable in a justice system that guarantees equal treatment under the law?

The flip side of this question is neighborhood competition. Earlier, we stated that stings to reduce prostitution in the adjacent Garfield neighborhood resulted in displacement of this activity to Coronado. Coronado residents complained about this displacement. This is a practical problem for the neighborhood agenda, but it is also a conceptual issue regarding the definition of community. Although Phoenix had preestablished neighborhood boundaries, this does not prevent the influence that activity in one community has on surrounding communities. To what extent can it be seen as an advantage of any community to displace problems to other locations?

The neighborhood probation initiatives in Phoenix will help open the door to these issues, and they will provide a way to understand them in practical terms. As a field experiment in community justice, the Phoenix neighborhood projects will provide a laboratory for the clarification of equal justice concerns.

Communities and Resources

The issue becomes sharpened when indigenous neighborhood resources are taken into account. The places that suffer most from crime and disorder are the ones that have the most trouble organizing resident resources to take on these issues. Coronado, for example, had a core of professional residents interested in the community who wrote grant proposals and engaged in other forms of community advocacy, and this laid the groundwork for a community-probation partnership. As poor as Coronado is, it is by no means the poorest or most crime-ridden neighborhood in Phoenix. What about these places? Can they offer the requisite level of indigenous resources to make community justice possible?

The community organization aspect of community justice may be an essential component of community justice. When the community unites and begins to communicate more, common goals and ideas surface and are able to be realized by a motivated group of people. As a citizen mentioned, when he suffered alone, nothing changed, but when he decided "to do" something about it and tell his story to the community, he found that others in the community shared his feelings. This allowed for group or collective problem solving to begin, which increased the likelihood for solutions to be found from community controls, both informal controls such as the neighborhood association and neighborhood watch and formal controls such as the police and probation department.

How can this kind of action be developed and sustained in the most hard-hit communities? In Coronado, an insurgence of grant funds was a catalyst for organizing the residents for action. It may be that a similar strategy of initial seed funding for multiproblem neighborhoods is a necessary element of community justice. The expansion of community probation into additional neighborhoods in Phoenix will provide some evidence on this question, as most of these newer initiatives are being conducted without the benefit of external philanthropy. If it turns out that the catalytic power of funding is an important element of change, then some way to reorient funds to this purpose will have to be found.

Partnerships and Accountability

In some respects, the partnerships established by the Coronado neighborhood probation staff with police, social services, and prominent residents are obvious, if not easy. It does not denigrate the significance of these partnerships to say that second-generation connections can be formed to further strengthen the community justice activity.

One component of the community justice model that probation officials feel is lacking at this time is an articulated victim's role. As Ebratt noted, there is a hotline that victims may call, but this does not constitute a significant emphasis on the victim. Many of the newer community justice projects have been built around a core active role for the crime victim, particularly in terms of the victim's input on sanctioning and the ability for the victim's voice to be heard through methods such as victim impact panels and restorative justice efforts.

Two developments have taken place within the community that suggest the community is realizing the importance of the role of the victim in the overall community justice model. An adult community court is being developed in Coronado, and it may provide a basis for a more active victim presence in the community justice effort. The judge in charge of the court has called on Coronado residents to participate in a forum to discuss how the courts can be community oriented. Moreover, a state resolution was passed allowing neighborhoods to be declared a victim of each crime that takes place in the community, but "we're still trying to figure out how all this works although the law is there," a community member said. Whether the new interest in victims will mirror the adversarial nature of traditional justice or embrace the problem-solving aims of community justice remains to be seen.

Evaluating Community Justice

As with most community justice programs, no evaluations of the impact of the Coronado Neighborhood Probation Office on the community, offenders, or victims have been conducted. It is commonly believed that longitudinal evaluations are necessary to determine the effectiveness of such a program. For the Coronado Neighborhood Probation Office, measures will need to examine crime rates, community satisfaction, victim satisfaction, and probationer (offender) satisfaction. Implied in the measurement of community satisfaction would be measures of the impact of the program on the quality of life in the community, such as residents' fear of crime.[2]

Nobody disputes the need for a formal evaluation of the community justice work in Phoenix. But an informal understanding of what has happened in Phoenix is already emerging, and staff and residents are enthusiastic alike about this new form of probation. As a resident explained, "We don't know what we would do without them [the probation staff]; at this point, we will not let them leave—Really!"

Notes

1. Two site visits were made to the Maricopa County Adult Probation Department and its neighborhood offices during

September and November, 1998. Numerous interviews were conducted with criminal justice personnel and community residents in Phoenix during this time.
2. During the summer of 1998, Jennifer Ferguson was hired by the Maricopa County Adult Probation Office as a research analyst to begin conducting research and evaluation of the Coronado program. According to Ferguson, ultimately they would like to produce evaluations of the community's knowledge of probation, perception of safety, increased employability of probationers, and other attributes of offenders.

References

Bursik, Robert J. and Harold G. Grasmick. 1993. *Neighborhoods and Crime: The Dimensions of Effective Community Control*. New York: Lexington Books.

Chavis, David M., Kien Lee, and Suzanne Merchlinsky. 1997. *National Cross-Site Evaluation of the Community Building Initiative*. Bethesda, MD: Cosmos.

Johnson, Jo Ann and C. Ashley. 1997. "Many Voices, One Song." *Phoenix Downtown*, January, p. 24.

Kelling, George L. 1992. "Measuring What Matters: A New Way of Thinking About Crime and Public Order." *City Journal*, Spring:21-33.

Kelling, George L. and Catherine M. Coles. 1996. *Fixing Broken Windows*. New York: Free Press.

Kennedy, David M. 1997. "Pulling Levers: Chronic Offenders, High-Crime Settings, and a Theory of Prevention." *Valparaiso University Law Review* 31:449-84.

Ruelas, Richard. 1997. "Serving Face to Face." *Arizona Republic*, June 1, pp. B1.

Sampson, Robert J. 1995. "The Community." Pp. 193-216 in *Crime*, edited by James Q. Wilson and Joan Petersilia. San Francisco: Institute for Contemporary Studies.

Sampson, Robert J. and Stephen Raudenbush. 1999. "Systematic Social Observation of Public Spaces: A New Look at Disorder in Urban Neighborhoods." *American Journal of Sociology* 105(3):603-51.

Senge, Peter. 1990. *The Fifth Discipline*. New York: Doubleday.

Skogan, Wesley G. 1990. *Disorder and Decline: Crime and the Spiral of Decay in American Neighborhoods*. New York: Free Press.

No location in the United States calls for citizen involvement more profoundly than does Vermont with its Community Reparative Boards. In most places where criminal justice has reached out to citizens, the level of participation is carefully constrained: citizens advise, citizens give feedback, or citizens provide support. In Vermont, involvement is much more basic: citizens decide and impose the sanctions.

Vermont's award-winning reparative boards are citizen tribunals that hear and dispose of so-called minor offenses: public intoxication and other disturbances of the peace, trespassing, theft, fraud, and so on. Several aspects of the Vermont approach set it apart from other citizen-based strategies, but the foremost difference is the level of control exercised by the citizens themselves. When a board reaches a decision, its determination is not advisory to any judicial group; rather, the board's determination becomes the actual sanction for the offender. This is a radical departure from even the most enthusiastic citizen participation approaches in other locations.

The reparative boards came about as a result of layers of dissatisfaction with the traditional justice system. One layer was the system itself, led by corrections officials who had grown tired of poor public opinion and had decided to try to change in ways that would increase the public acceptance of correctional activity. The other layer was the public, about whom studies made an interesting point: they were less interested in a system that "got tough" than they were in having a system that "made sense." The corrections people spent a period of time trying to understand why the public was so dissatisfied. What came out of that process was a call for change, the centerpiece of which was to expand the involvement of citizens in the sanctioning process.

One of the keys to effective community involvement is to reach out to the *relevant community*. Because the offenses covered by the reparative boards include the kinds of crimes that create community disorder, their entire community is affected by these offenses. In this way, the community board members, who represent the views and values of the larger community, truly stand in for the larger community that suffers harm from these offenses. Although there is no obligation that these board members try to figure out what the community wants, by virtue of their status as residents, they represent community views and interests.

But the community is not the only participant in the reparative boards. All *stakeholders* to the offense—victim, offender, and family members— are given a voice in the board hearings. This enables the board to expand the perspectives on the offense and the offender while also opening the door to hear creative solutions to deal with particular offenses. The idea that a sanctioning board becomes an opportunity for an exchange between representatives of the community and the transgressor transforms the rote ceremonies of justice in the typical courtroom into a conversation about responsibility, accountability, and harm. Stakeholders do not have to leave the pursuit of their interests to professional representatives, something that can be hit or miss in practice, but instead are free to speak for themselves.

Power sharing between the state and the involved citizen, under this approach, is not just an idea or an intention, it is a fact. Vermonters who offend have a chance to speak for themselves about the meaning of their offense and how they understand its consequences; Vermonters who are offended against have a chance to talk about what happened to them and its impact on their lives. But the key is that the power to decide how to reach closure about the problem lies entirely with the board. In this way, power is not merely shared, it is shifted.

The Vermont approach has won awards because it is so revolutionary in its rearrangement of the relationships between state, victim, offender, and citizen. In the usual model, advocates speak to judges while victims, offenders, and interested citizens watch and wait to see if they are called to testify. The Vermont model removes the advocates and attorneys and puts the offender in direct response to the citizens. If community justice cannot emerge from this arrangement, it is hard to see how it can emerge from any new strategy.

Chapter Three

The Offender/ Community Encounter

Stakeholder Involvement in the Vermont Community Reparative Boards

David R. Karp

The victim's role in community and restorative justice is a central one and has received much attention in the literature. In particular, studies have examined both the ideal and the reality of interactional dynamics between victims and offenders (Umbreit 1994) as well as victims and community members (Hudson et al. 1996). This is an appropriate focus for community justice. Nevertheless, the relationship of the offender to the community is also central to community justice. It is here that we find the possibility of offender recompense, reintegration, and acceptance.

This case study examines the offender/community relationship and is guided by a very basic question: What happens when community members confront offenders in response to their crimes?

In contemporary criminal justice, relations between community members and offenders are minimized. Indeed, they are severed almost completely when the offender is incarcerated. Typically, community members are given no formal role in the decision-making process following arrest and have little knowledge of the offender's criminal status even when the offender remains a community resident. The central reasons why community/offender relations are minimized in contemporary justice practice are (1) to protect offenders' rights to privacy and (2) to prevent community members from taking the law into their own hands either directly through vigilantism or indirectly through ostracism and discrimination (e.g., employers who refuse to hire offenders).

The victims' movement has lobbied successfully for one significant change in contemporary practice. Arguing that the community has a right to know if offenders have been released into its neighborhoods, victims' advocates have encouraged state legislatures to enact Megan's Law, requiring that residents be notified when a sex offender is released from prison. Advocates argue that this knowledge enables residents to better protect themselves from the risks posed by these offenders. Sometimes, however, communities have engaged in vigilantism in order to drive the offender from the community. In Washington state, for example, a sex offender's house was burned down the week he returned from prison (Associated Press 1993).

With Megan's Law, the community gains knowledge of the offenders' whereabouts, and in some local areas, educational forums are created to provide the community with acceptable strategies for risk reduction (Finn 1997). But this change does not create formal settings for offender/community interaction, in which each side gets to voice concerns and listen to the other's perspective. Criminal offenders are deviants in the sense that they have violated behavioral standards expected of community members. Thus, others in the community are naturally concerned about offenders' future compliance with these standards. In community justice, these concerns are not dismissed or displaced by the criminal justice apparatus. Instead, forums are created to bring these stakeholders to the table.

Such forums are the defining feature of the Vermont Community Reparative Boards. What, then, do community members and offenders say to one another in such settings? Do they use this forum as an opportunity for shaming and ostracism? Are offenders cooperative or belligerent or withdrawn? How do community members communicate to offenders that their behavior was unacceptable and needs to change? How much do community members agree with one another, and how do they manage disagreement among themselves?

The heart of community justice is in the use of informal social control (Clear and Karp 1999). Community justice relies on the capacity of community residents to address crime problems themselves, without relinquishing this responsibility to the criminal justice system. What we must understand is how such processes of informal control are undertaken. We must examine closely the intuitive strategies of residents when they confront offenders. These are charged interactional encounters, ones that we often wish to avoid. I am struck by a comment made by Erving Goffman 39 years ago:

> When normals and stigmatized do in fact enter one another's immediate presence, especially when they then attempt to sustain a joint conversational encounter, there occurs one of the primal scenes of sociology; for, in many cases, these moments will be the ones when the causes and effects of stigma must be directly confronted by both sides. (Goffman 1963:13)

So what happens when community members confront norm violators in an informal conversational encounter? What are they compelled to say? What strategies do they use to negotiate their way through these tense, ambiguous, even adversarial moments? As with other community justice programs, such moments have been created by the Vermont Department of Corrections (VDOC). In Vermont's reparative board program, community volunteers serve on boards that meet with adult offenders to negotiate terms of reparation to victims and to the community.

Overview of the Vermont Community Reparative Boards

Vermont is not a high-crime state. It has no large urban centers, and it has a fairly homogeneous population and a violent crime rate that is one-third the national average (Vermont Department of Corrections 1998). Nevertheless, Vermont has followed the trends elsewhere in punishing criminals by giving prison sentences more frequently and for longer durations. In 1991, its prison system was at 191% capacity (Perry and Gorczyk 1997). Because the state budget is relatively small, paying for new prison construction could not be hidden by creative accounting. It was clear that a larger prison budget would cut directly into the education budget. A creative correctional staff recognized that its choices were limited: "Meet the increased demand with level resources produces continuous decline in quality, resulting in even greater dissatisfaction, or disaster. Or, reinvent the business" (Perry and Gorczyk 1997:27). On that premise, Corrections Commissioner John Gorczyk and his staff began a formal examination of the correctional system and its relationship to the public interest. Their reinvention began with a public survey conducted by John Doble Research Associates, Inc.

The Doble Survey

John Doble's (1994) report on public beliefs and attitudes about crime and criminal justice in Vermont is extensive, and only a few points will be summarized here. First, a majority of Vermonters did not believe the correctional system was doing a good job, in general, or with regard to rehabilitation. They believed incarcerated offenders were not engaged in activities that were beneficial to the community or to themselves. Instead, they believed that "our jails and prisons are schools for prisoners that turn inmates into hardened criminals." Despite this poor assessment, Vermonters saw little alternative for violent offenders: 93% of Vermonters agreed that violent offenders should be incarcerated. Vermonters were also dissatisfied with the major alternative for offenders: probation and parole. Sixty-one percent believed the probation and parole system was not properly "keeping tabs on offenders to make sure they don't commit more crimes." The same percentage believed that probation and parole were not successful in rehabilitating offenders.

Although Vermonters exhibited much consensus about the need to incarcerate violent offenders, this did not extend to nonviolent offenders. For them, 95% favored restitution and community service. Attitudes with regard to drunk drivers were particularly interesting. Vermonters supported three distinct objectives: (1) community service to rectify the harm caused by the offense (93% in favor), (2) alcohol abuse assessment and treatment to rehabilitate problem drinkers (93% in favor), and (3) forums for having "drunk drivers talk to mothers whose children were killed by drunk drivers so they'll realize how serious their crime is" (87% in favor). Eighty-two percent of Vermonters preferred having drunk drivers do 90 days of community service along with alcohol treatment rather than spend 30 days in jail. From these survey items, we find significant public support for correctional objectives that include (a) restoration of victims and communities and (b) rehabilitation of offenders that includes their acknowledgment of the harm caused by their offenses.

Doble also examined the idea of community reparative boards. From this we learn a third correctional objective from Vermonters: They want significant citizen involvement in the decision-making process with offenders—they want an offender/community relationship. Ninety-two percent of Vermonters supported the idea of having citizen volunteers work with judges "to oversee the sentence of selected nonviolent offenders." The original vision for these boards was captured in the exact wording of the survey item:

> One idea is to set up "Community Reparations Boards" where citizen-volunteers would work with a judge to determine and oversee the sentence of selected nonviolent offenders. Instead of prison, offenders would have to complete activities determined by the Board that might include some, or all, of the following: unpaid community service-work such as cutting brush; restitution or paying back the victim of the crime; house arrest with electronic monitoring; writing a letter of apology to the victim; successfully completing a counseling program about making key decisions in life; and successfully completing a drug or alcohol rehabilitation program. How do you feel about using Community Boards to determine and supervise the unpaid work and other activities of selected offenders instead of sending them to prison?

Although Vermonters were enthusiastic about the idea of community boards, their support was limited to nonviolent offenders. The findings clearly showed that Vermonters believed prison was still appropriate for violent offenders. Almost no one believed a rapist or armed robber should appear before a community board in lieu of incarceration.

At the time of the survey, no community boards existed: nonviolent offenders were sentenced to probation or prison. Reparative boards were designed as part of a larger strategy of programming that would provide the courts with meaningful alternatives to incarceration. The community boards might better address the concerns Vermonters had with traditional probation and to meet the public's wish for victim and community restoration as well as citizen involvement.

Sentencing Tracks and Reparative Probation

Vermont's reinvention corresponded closely with the results of the Doble survey. Corrections was reorganized along two "sentencing tracks." In so doing, VDOC considerably expanded the repertoire of sentencing options available to judges. Each track has a separate underlying purpose; thus, an offender's sentence would follow along each track. The first track is "risk management." Here, corrections managers were concerned with public safety and the need for incapacitation. Along this track are a range of options from intensive supervision of offenders in the community to incarceration. Insofar as rehabilitation corresponds with public protection, this track also includes treatment options. The second track is "reparative." Here, the concern is for repairing the damage caused by the offense. The options range from orders of restitution and apology to work service by incarcerated offenders. Within this track is "reparative probation," a legal status that requires offenders to appear before Community Reparative Boards and comply with an agreement negotiated in order to be released from this probationary status. Former director of the reparative program Michael Dooley (1995) summarized the goals of the reparative track:

> Specific purposes and goals of the reparative program are to implement the restorative model of criminal justice; to bring Vermonters actively into the criminal justice sanctions process as volunteers; to make Vermont's criminal justice system more responsive to the crime-related needs of victims and communities; and to address broader administrative and systemic needs for economy in the execution of the corrections mission. (p. 31)

A Typical Case

To illustrate the community justice process, I will trace the events for one offender as they proceeded from arrest to appearance before the community board. On the night of May 25, 1998, John Burns (pseudonym) was arrested for driving under the influence of alcohol in the city of Rutland. The arresting officer had observed Burns weaving erratically and pass through a red light. After pulling Burns over, the officer questioned him from outside the driver's side window. At this point, Burns accidentally rolled the vehicle forward twice. The second time took the vehicle forward 25 feet until it hit a utility pole. When the case appeared before the court, the defendant was found guilty of DWI (driving while intoxicated) and sentenced to reparative probation with the condition that he "shall actively participate in and complete the Reparative Probation Program at the discretion of and to the full satisfaction of the Reparative Coordinator."

All reparative cases are first adjudicated in court. This is not a diversionary program. Defendants may refuse to appear before reparative boards, leaving it to the judge to determine the specific conditions of the sentence. Otherwise, judges may impose their own conditions (such as an alcohol assessment or restitution to victims) and the reparative board conditions, in which the community board determines the specific terms of the reparative agreement. When a case is assigned to reparative probation, it is forwarded to the Department of Corrections Court and Reparative Services Unit within the local jurisdiction.

A reparative team (which includes correctional staff and volunteer roles such as a victim liaison and a community service opportunities developer) is responsible for managing the reparative caseload of the local boards. Responsibilities include (a) conducting an intake interview with offenders that orients them to the program, (b) processing paperwork and acting as liaison to the court, attorneys, other interested parties, and community justice centers, (c) scheduling the offender to appear before the board, (d) identifying and contacting victims or other parties who may wish to attend the reparative board hearing, (e) recruiting and coordinating training of volunteers for board membership and other volunteer roles associated with the program, (f) developing reparative resources, such as community service opportunities, family group conferencing, victim impact panels, and other activities relevant to reparative contracts, and (g) monitoring offender compliance with the reparative agreement.

The drunk driving offense of John Burns is one of many types of offenses on the reparative caseload. Other typical offenses include vandalism, retail theft, writing bad checks, furnishing alcohol to minors, possession of alcohol by minors, marijuana possession, and other nonviolent offenses. Determination of the target offender population is based on a risk management protocol, described by VDOC as "the 42-box model." This refers to a 6×7 table used to rank an offender according to their supervision needs based on the severity of the offense and the risk for reoffense. Severe offenses, even if a first time, do not qualify for reparative probation. Some moderate offenses, such as simple assault, might qualify if it is a first offense but not if it is a repetition. In general, low-severity offenses are targeted for reparative probation. Sometimes judges will send cases to the boards that fall outside the target population, but in general, the boards handle relatively minor cases and do not see more serious offenders such as violent offenders or sex offenders.

John Burns was arrested on May 24, 1998, sentenced on June 29, and appeared before the local reparative board on August 25. When offenders appear before a community board, they will come face to face with a small group of volunteers from the local community. In general, between three and five board members will be present for a hearing. Board members are not a perfect representation of the local community. First, because the time commitment is significant both in regard to member training and regular attendance, it is not likely that a perfect representation could ever be realized. Second, although it is currently a goal of VDOC to increase representativeness, the initial recruitment strategy did not select for this. Instead, they used a leader nomination method. Several prominent local leaders were identified by VDOC in each jurisdiction. These leaders were then asked to nominate people they believed would be capable and interested in serving on a reparative board. From this pool, the initial board members were recruited. Subsequently, recruitment has functioned by word of mouth and primarily through active recruitment by the reparative team. The latter have been specifically charged with increasing the representativeness of the boards to include, for example, more low-income community members and ex-offenders who have successfully completed the reparative program.

Prospective board members generally observe board hearings before joining them. When they do become board members, they must participate in 15 hours of training within the first six months. This training includes an introduction to restorative justice principles and various restorative models such as victim-offender mediation, circle sentencing, and family group conferencing. Board members participate in role-playing exercises and other activities designed to develop good communication skills in their interactions with offenders, victims, and other board members. In addition, ongoing board members are expected to participate in seven hours of in-service training each year. Recently, VDOC has developed protocols for board self-evaluation.

On August 25, 1998, John Burns arrived at Rutland's Department of Corrections' Court and Reparative Services Unit (CRSU) (Vermont's version of a local probation office) office to appear before the Tuesday evening panel. The larger towns and cities in Vermont have too many cases for one board to handle, and boards have grown and subdivided into two or more panels with different members. At this particular panel, four board members were present, three women and one man (across the state, board membership is 60% male and 40% female). As of December 1998, there were 41 boards operating in 21 townships, with a pool of 260 board members.

These boards had processed more than 2,800 cases from their inception in November 1995 through 1998.

Boards vary as to how they manage a hearing, how long they will spend discussing the case, and even how they will respond to like cases. Nevertheless, each board is expected to pursue five goals:[1]

1. Victims and affected parties describe the impact of the offenders' behavior.

2. Offenders make amends to victims and affected parties.

3. Offenders make amends to the community.

4. Offenders demonstrate healthy behaviors and learn ways to avoid reoffending.

5. The community offers reintegration.

These goals closely correspond to the Karp and Clear (2000) Community Justice Model (see Exhibit 1.3 in Chapter 1 for a full explication of the model). The first three goals follow the reparative pathway, and the latter two follow the reintegrative. Vermont's board program is generally representative of the integrity model in all four of its process dimensions: a correctional system that has made itself more accessible and garnered significant citizen involvement while pursuing both reparative and reintegrative agendas.

The Rutland panel began its hearing by introducing themselves to John Burns and reviewing the formal documents of the case. They then asked the offender to talk about himself—where he works, where he lives, etc.—and to give a full account of the drunk driving incident. All boards begin with such information gathering, laying the groundwork for negotiating a reparative agreement that is specifically relevant to the case. This board then asked the offender to leave the room while board members discussed the case among themselves. Several boards adhere to this closed door procedure, whereas others proceed directly to a discussion of the contract with the offender present. VDOC had originally recommended this recess discussion but has subsequently decided that the procedure is problematic and runs counter to the restorative philosophy. Some boards have dropped the recess, and others have maintained it. Briefly, some boards like the recess because they want to maintain a united front before an offender (voicing disagreement with each other only behind closed doors), they want to maintain a sense of authority and confidence before the offender, and they do not want any board members placed at risk because they had advocated more punitive terms than the others. However, other boards have relinquished the recess because they believe it reduced the trust between the board and the offenders and disempowered the offenders by undermining their active role in the decision-making process.

The centerpiece of the board hearing is the negotiation of the agreement. Here, each of the four goals is identified and addressed. The board did not identify a victim in this case, so no terms were established on this point. In other cases, restitution and letters of apology are common. Creatively, some boards have identified the arresting officer as a victim when the offender was rude or resisted arrest. Then they might ask the offender to write an apology to the officer. The Burns board advocated 50 hours of community service but left it to the offender to identify the type of service at a later date. To fulfill the goal of having the offender learn about the consequences of his behavior, the board asked the offender to complete two tasks. The first was to attend a one-hour Encare session, in which emergency room nurses describe horror stories of other drunk driving cases. Second, the offender was asked to write a three-page essay on "the importance of laws in the community—why what you did was wrong and what would happen if everyone did that." Finally, to fulfill the last requirement of seeking ways to avoid reoffense, the board required that the offender take a one-day defensive driving class and obtain an alcohol assessment.

John Burns agreed to the terms of the reparative contract. This hearing lasted approximately 30 minutes; others sometimes take less but more often run between 40 minutes and one hour. Like all other reparative probationers, he had 90 days to complete the reparative tasks. Otherwise, he would be in violation and would either go back to the board for renegotiation or back to court. Some, but not all, boards ask offenders to return after 30 or 60 days (or both) for a brief check-in on their progress and sometimes also a closure meeting at the end of the 90 days.

The Vermont Video Project

Between August 1998 and July 1999, I videotaped 53 reparative board hearings, covering the various boards across the state. See Karp and Walther (2001) for details on the methodology of this study. From these observations and discussions with VDOC personnel and board members, I provide below some analyses of the board process, each of which is driven by the basic question, What do community members do when meeting face to face with a criminal offender? By no means is this an exhaustive listing of possible encounters. Instead, I examine four common occurrences: (1) attempts to establish common ground, (2) affirmations of normative standards, (3) responses to offender denials of responsibility, and (4) disagreements between board members about ideal contracts.

Common Ground

The relational dynamic between board members and offenders is quite different from those between judges and offenders. The symbolism of the court—the bench, the flag, the robes, the gavel—emphasizes that the judge is a representative of the state: distant, objective, authoritative, powerful. Board members wear casual dress, sit around a table, meet in nondescript community rooms in libraries, town halls, CRSU offices, or police stations. Though some boards are more formal than others, they all seem to prioritize friendliness and civility; the offender is made to feel welcome. Boards introduce themselves by name to the offender and convey to the offender that they are volunteers, rather than paid staff of VDOC. It is clear, however, that there remains much social distance between many of the offenders and the board members. Board members tend to be older (with many retirees serving on them), better educated, and more articulate. Nevertheless, it seems important to board members to find some common ground with the offender, board members stating, for example, that they live on the same road or attended the same school or know a member of the offender's family. The idea, it seems, is to make the offender feel comfortable and therefore become a more willing participant in the process. More fundamentally, the purpose is to remind one another that each is a member of the same community, linked together in consequential ways.

One illustration of an attempt to establish common ground comes from the same Rutland panel that heard the case of John Burns. Similarly, Neal Gresham (pseudonym) appeared before the board for a DWI conviction. Typically, in such cases, board members will ask how the offender is managing without a license (which is invariably suspended by the judge after such convictions).[2] While pursuing this line of inquiry, one board member found his chance to find common ground:

Board Member 1:	How do you get to work?
Offender:	My friend, we both work up at Middlebury.
Board Member 2:	Who are you working for up in Middlebury?

Offender:	[Name of contractor.] They're out of Boston.
Board Member 2:	Yeah, what are you doing up there?
Offender:	Slate roofing.
Board Member 2:	Which building do you work on now?
Offender:	On the college. It's a huge building.
Board Member 2:	Yeah, I'm working on the same building.
Offender:	You are?!?
Board Member 2:	Yeah. The science building.
Offender:	Yup! That's where it is.
Board Member 2:	I thought I'd seen you before.

Two consequences seemed to follow from this brief interaction. First, the offender immediately relaxed, smiling for the first time in the hearing, feeling like he could identify with at least one person on the board. Second, there was an implication that his future behavior could be monitored. He might, in fact, see this board member again soon on the job. These points emphasize the two fundamental qualities of informal control: that it is undertaken by members of the community in unregulated settings (informal) and that it may indeed be undertaken (control).

Norm Affirmation

I have suggested that board members attempt to establish common ground in part because they want to emphasize that they are, offenders included, all members of the same community. In almost every board I have observed, board members have also tried to make the case to offenders that such membership entails a responsibility to conform to the normative standards of the community, that the offender's violation is not a private matter but one of great concern to a community of interdependent residents.

It appears that board members are deeply motivated to reaffirm the moral order of the community. The offender has violated a community trust, and this trust can only be reestablished when the norms are reaffirmed by board members and the offender. Most important, the board members will try to get the offender to see the offense as they do: as an abrogation of the community code and an aberration of the offenders which they will not repeat. Again, I draw on the ideas of Goffman (1967):

The suspected person thus shows that he is thoroughly capable of taking the role of the others toward his own activity, . . . that the rules of conduct which he appears to have broken are still sacred, real, and unweakened. An offensive act may arouse anxiety about the ritual code; the offender allays this anxiety by showing that both the code and he as an upholder of it are still in working order. (pp. 21-2)

This process is illuminated in three examples. The first involved a particularly minor offense. The offender, Rick Lamott (pseudonym), had been arrested for driving without a license, which had been suspended because he had failed to pay his registration fees.

Board Member:	Rick, do you understand why—this on the surface seems like a pretty innocuous or minor type of an offense—I mean we're takin' your time and our time and the Department of Corrections' time to deal with this thing, which is something you could have taken care of two or three years ago by paying simply what you owed and makin' right what you'd done. Do you understand why we're making such an issue out of this?
Offender:	Probably because it's been a repetitive sort of thing. I can understand where I ignored my fines—I did. I'm more than happy to pay them now.
Board Member:	I mean you wouldn't come into my house and steal something and break the law doing that, would you?
Offender:	No.
Board Member:	Yet you're willfully breaking the laws here. I mean a law applies to me and you whether you like it or not and whether I like it or not, and I think that's the point we need to get across with you today. You can't just selectively say, "Oh, the heck with it, I'm not gonna pay the fine, or I don't have time, or I didn't think about it." You gotta pay attention to this stuff cause you're a member of the community and that's your responsibility.
Offender:	Yup, I understand that—now. Now that I'm older and I've got a daughter and everything.

First, the board member establishes that the offender shares the same moral universe by inquiring about his willingness to engage in more significant criminal activity ("You wouldn't come into my house and steal something"). Clearly, this is a rhetorical question, but he did wait for the offender to reply in order to gain that reassurance. Second, he reminds the offender of his responsibilities as a member of the community, responsibilities that are equally shared by all members. To underscore this point, as part of the contract with the offender, he was asked to write a three-page essay on "Why I should obey the laws of my community."

In a second illustration, the obligation of communal membership is coupled with an articulation of the harm caused by the offender's behavior. In this case, the offender had supplied his two teen-aged sons with a case of beer and wine coolers so they might go drinking with other neighborhood friends.

| Board Member: | The next thing that we need to talk about is the fact that, being a member of a community, which you are, supported by the rest of us, in terms of all kinds of things, that you have let us all down. Because one of the problems that we have, all of us, is controlling kids who get involved in drugs and alcohol. We spend a lot of money and a lot of time on it. It's very worrisome for us . . . when parents who have children the age of yours are talking to them about abstinence and staying in control and so forth, and here you are, an adult down the street who is saying to your kids, "Go ahead, drink all you want." You're working at cross-purposes and I don't think that's very fair of you. And I think you've got to do something to acknowledge that you've failed to hold up your end of the bargain as a member of the community and to do something to make amends for that. |

Thus, the norm affirmation process is closely linked with the harm caused by violations of the normative code. Moreover, board members seek acknowledgment from offenders that the codes are respected by them and will be observed in the future. By affirming the norms, the board members allow for the offense to be construed as exceptional, and that once the harmfulness has been fully considered, it will not be repeated.

As a final illustration of the norm affirmation process, an articulation of harm is coupled with an attempt to establish common ground. In this case, a 20-year-old woman was convicted of possession of beer and reckless driving (but not convicted of DWI because she was on medication and the breath test was voided).

Board Member: This group takes alcohol-related crimes pretty seriously. It's a huge problem in this town. It's a huge problem in this state. You've heard about the guy who's arrested 27 times for alcohol, kills two or three people before they finally get him off the road. We're not trying to pick on you. We're trying to get you to understand that it may have sounded like you just squealed your tires, but it was a real bad judgment call. You're a young person. It was a bad judgment call for you to be on the road at all, for you to take either one of those substances [and] be driving. But to add insult to injury, you had to take them both. That's something that the board wants to get you to understand real clearly; I think it was worthy of a DWI. I don't want to retry your case. I want you to really clearly think about the fact that pulling this kind of thing again, you're gonna be [given a DWI]. [Pause] The one thing I did not do at the beginning was introduce ourselves. It probably would have been nice if you had a clue as to who you were talking to. I'm [name] and I've lived in Randolph forever. [Other board members introduce themselves.]

What was interesting in this encounter was the board member's apparent need to reinforce her normative claims by verifying the board's status as local volunteers and by balancing an authoritative judgment with an attempt to reach out and create familiarity and connection. It is these kinds of expressions that are unique to the boards. Judges often make similar normative claims, but they cannot achieve the same level of rapport.

In the cases that I have observed, what is rare is when these norm affirmation strategies *do not* occur. In one instance, the case involved another 20-year-old found guilty of possessing alcohol. Apparently, he had been walking home with some beer in his backpack when he was stopped and searched by the arresting officer. As the offender pointed out, he "was stopped seven months too soon." This board did not condone the behavior but was unable to articulate what harm the offender had caused, what norm needed reaffirmation. In a second case, the board was persuaded by the offender's account that the offender, in fact, was the victim and had been acting in self-defense (in a confrontation with a teen-aged stepson). Once again, this board found it difficult to identify the harm caused by the offender. I am not suggesting here that, in reality, a norm was or wasn't violated, but to explain why the typical norm affirmation strategies were not applied in these cases. When boards do not effectively articulate the harm caused by offenders or do not believe the offender to be culpable, they do not seek to affirm the normative order.

Denials of Responsibility

Board hearings are negotiated events in two senses. An agreement must be reached that the offender will sign and comply with. But this practical matter is the pretext for a more subtle negotiation of the burden of responsibility. Offenders, presumably, are motivated to minimize their sense of guilt and obligation. They would rather place the blame elsewhere and also have the board agree with such a version of events. In one case mentioned above, the board, in fact, did come to share the offender's view (quite in contrast to the judge) and consequently negotiated a very "light" agreement. More generally, however, board members are compelled by the need to affirm the moral order and, therefore, wish to hold offenders accountable, maximizing their sense of guilt and obligation.

Clearly, there is a dramatic imbalance of power in these negotiations. The offender is likely to acquiesce on all fronts, passively accepting the terms as devised by the board.[3] They generally do not have the verbal skills to defend themselves well, and often they recognize that any such attempts might be seen as uncooperative, which might lead to a more punitive contract. It is generally in their interest to be polite and agree with board members at every turn. Those boards that deliberate terms during a recess exacerbate this imbalance of power. In the case of John Burns, for example, when he returned to the table, the chairperson declared, "Okay, John, we have come to an agreement." They certainly did not come to that agreement with the offender.

John Burns, you will remember, was the drunk driver who managed to roll his car into a telephone pole when the arresting officer was standing nearby. He is also an example of an offender who tried to persuade the board that he was not culpable.

Offender:	I had three beers that night. . . . I had three beers and I drove straight. If you notice, it doesn't say anything about swerving.
Board Member 1:	[Skimming police report] Yeah it does, absolutely.
Offender:	Probably because I was looking in the rearview mirror.
Board Member 2:	So you think this whole thing—You've been treated unfairly. The cop screwed up the report; you weren't really drunk.
Offender:	I wasn't *drunk* drunk. I had three beers.
Board Member 2:	Well, actually, we tend to take the policeman's attitude at face value.
Offender:	I understand.
Board Member 2:	And we also take this offense that you were charged with as being the most serious offense that comes before this board. Even if there's no accident, even if there's no injury. It's not a victimless crime.
Board Member 3:	The other thing, too, John, is that you don't want to take responsibility for your actions. You've given us all excuses so far.
Offender:	[Suddenly shame-faced and beet red] No, I've taken responsibility. I know that I drove that night and that was a bad thing to do. I've never done that before, and never will again.

The board refuses to accept John's version of events while reaffirming the normative standard. What was fascinating in this interaction was the immediate reversal undertaken by the offender when he realized the board would not accept his account. He shifts from a claim that he was neither drunk nor swerving to agreeing that he had done a "bad thing." Initially defiant, when confronted directly about his excuses, he blushed in embarrassment and shame. The strategy used by the board to get the offender to take responsibility was straightforward: they did not accept his denial and emphasized their own seriousness with which they treat the incident.

In another incident, a board member uses a strategy that calls attention to the harmfulness of the offense. In this case, a young woman, Melanie Vandergross (pseudonym), was convicted of a simple assault. As the board discovered, she had been arguing with her mother-in-law and punched her in the mouth. The victim did not attend the board hearing. The following interaction took place after one board member suggested that the offender might need to write a letter of apology to the victim. Up until this point, the offender denied responsibility for the assault, claiming that she had been justly provoked.

Offender:	It sounds horrible, but I don't know right now if I am really willing to write her a letter [of apology]. I mean, I can lie to you and say, "Oh yeah, great." But honestly, really, I don't really think I'm ready to do that.
Board Member:	Let me ask you a question on a slightly different level—a different approach. Your eldest child was a witness to this.
Offender:	Right.
Board Member:	Seems to me the child is also a victim. You acted out in anger, rather violent anger, in front of an innocent child against that child's grandparent.
[Six minutes later]	
Offender:	What happened was horrible. And I wish we could take it all back. And I would be willing to write them a letter or call them up or have them over for dinner.

The board's focus had been on articulating the harm caused by the offense. However, its strategy until this exchange had been to get the offender to see the incident from the point of view of the mother-in-law. But the offender's anger prevented her from being able to engage in this role-taking. The board member then asked her to see the incident from the perspective of her two-year-old daughter. Apparently, this was effective, for a dramatic reversal in her willingness to apologize occurred just a few minutes later. Through this role-taking, the offender saw the incident in a new light, which enabled her to see its harmful effects and accept the obligation to make amends. These incidents illustrate two primary strategies used by board members to offset denials of responsibility: (1) point-blank refusals to accept offenders' excuses, and (2) finding creative ways to illuminate the harmfulness of the conduct such as through role-taking.

Civil Disagreement and Conflicting Justice Philosophies

Boards vary from one to the next. Some are conservative and formal, emphasizing a strict adherence to rules of order. Others are liberal and informal, rarely referring to official mandates and procedures. Some lean toward punitive, adopting the role of "citizen judges" in order to "sentence" the offender, albeit in a restorative manner. Others are rather therapeutic, adopting a "citizen counselor" role, ready to discuss at length the offender's difficult past and generate agreements that will be rehabilitative. Some boards believe 10 hours of community service is a norm that should rarely be exceeded. Others happily assign 40 or more.

Of course, such tendencies vary within as well as between the boards, and members have plenty of material about which to disagree. Some distrust the offenders' account, thinking they are guilty of more than the offenders claim and perhaps more than to what the conviction alludes. Others are more willing to ally themselves with the offenders, distrusting the court conviction, believing, at least, that they will get the more honest account than the police report.

The Vermont boards are predicated on a community justice philosophy. Their mandate is to generate contracts that will, as Commissioner Gorczyk likes to assert, "add value" by restoring victims and communities through restitution and community service. The boards are also expected to facilitate the reintegration of offenders by helping them to understand their role as community members (by understanding the consequences of their behavior) and to find better ways to manage their lives (strategies to help them avoid reoffending). Community justice, however, is a new justice philosophy that is distinct from the more familiar models of retribution and rehabilitation. But board members bring these familiar models to the table even as they try to embrace and apply the newer concepts. The restorative component often becomes fused with the retributive: the community service is construed as a punishment. The reintegrative component often becomes fused with the rehabilitative: the focus turns to treatment as the sole vehicle for reintegration.

Rarely do boards have the opportunity to reflect on the various justice models and their implications. They are volunteer practitioners with caseloads, and their actions reflect a mixture of traditional and contemporary justice philosophies. Occasionally, disagreements over what the offender contract should look like are rooted in more fundamental tensions between these different philosophies. In the following discussion, conducted quite civilly and with the offender present, board members became entangled by a seemingly practical matter: How many hours of community service should be assigned?

Board Member 1:   I'm on a completely different wavelength. I think what you are talking about is how much we give him [number of hours]. I think what we should be talking about is what he gives us. Therefore, it has nothing to do with time, it has to do with the quality of his time.

Board Member 2:   I think time's a factor, too.

Board Member 1:   No, I don't think so.

Board Member 3:   Well, we have to deal with something concrete in order to write a contract and have an agreement about what is going to be done. Because quality we can't know about or he can't know about it until he does it. And even when he does it, we're not necessarily going to know what the quality was. We may never know that.

Board Member 4:   The point is, is his experience going to have some transformational effect? [To offender:] This isn't punishment. This is an attempt to transform your attitude about alcohol and children. [To others:] The quantity of time isn't important, and how he comes back and reports to [us] will indicate the degree to which it is taken.

Board Member 2:   Are we saying that 20 hours would have more motivational factor than 30?

Board Member 4:   No, not necessarily. We think that 20 will certainly, at least by the time we see him next time, have created enough experience that he can report back to us what it means to him. It will either be persuasive or not.

Board Member 1: Let's set up a hypothetical. The hypothetical is that I suggested that he put in some time—I said 5. I could have said 1, I could have said 20. It doesn't matter. And he comes back and reports that he has become an assistant scout leader working with young kids. And he's absolutely enthralled with it. And we realize that here's a guy who is going to spend a lot of time for the rest of his life invested in community service. What's the point of asking him to do six more hours. He's accomplished what we wanted him to accomplish, which is a sense of responsibility to the community. It has nothing to do with whether he puts in 10 minutes or 10 hours. So I think that if we want to say, "We value your transformation," then we have to do it by what we say. If we say, "We want you to bundle in 20 hours and we don't care what your attitude is, we just want you to put in 20 hours," then we are talking out both sides of our mouth.

Board Member 2: I can't wholly agree with that. What I heard [Board Member 3] say is that in fairness to him, we need to establish in the coming 60 days what the maximum of our expectations will be so that 30 days from now we don't hand him something that is unfair.

Board Member 3: That's true. And I also think we can hope it will be transforming. But it may not be. We can't say, "Well, you weren't transformed, you weren't converted, you weren't this or that, so back to jail or court you go." I don't think we can do that. We can't dictate what the psychological results of their being here [will be]. We can hope to come up with a good contract that will be helpful to you [offender], but there's the other segment of the reparative to the community. There is a give back. People are here to give back to the community. It may be difficult and they may not like everything they do and it may not teach them anything, but they have given something back. Doing community service gives back to the community even if, in the end, the per-

> son isn't changed. I don't think we can dictate that if they're not changed and they don't take some test that proves to us they've changed, they fail.

This is an unusually rich and reflective exchange during a board hearing. What began as an attempt to specify the number of work hours evolved into a profound discussion of the purpose of the board. The first board member challenged the board to think about the assignment of hours in a new way. The focus, he suggested, should not be on the number of hours, with the assumption that their determination is directly proportional to offense severity. Instead, he argued that community service is successful only when the offender becomes truly engaged in its performance. This engagement cannot be determined by the number of hours. Instead, he had argued previously, the offender ought to do just a few hours initially but find something rewarding. Then he should come back to the board, persuade the board that the service was transformative, thereby reassuring the board that the moral order has been affirmed— that the offender is a citizen now invested in the quality of community life and not a threat to it. In this interpretation, and I may indeed be inferring too much, the proposal is consistent with both the reparative and reintegrative trajectories of community justice.

There is an element to this proposal, however, that merges the reintegrative with the rehabilitative ("This isn't punishment. This is an attempt to transform your attitude about alcohol and children."). And it is this fusion, I suspect, that made other board members resistant to the proposal. With a rehabilitative focus, the board members become charged with treating the offender, and the service work is a treatment modality. This is a distinct shift from using the service work as a means to gain reassurance from the offender that he will abide by the community code to using service as a vehicle for psychological change that board members are little able to assess.

The alternative approach suggested in this exchange is a clear specification of the service work hours, partly in fairness to the offender who might want his tasks clearly enumerated and partly in fairness to the community that is in need of concrete reparations for the harm caused by the offense. In this discussion, no one takes a retributive stance—that the service work ought to be costly to the offender in exact proportion to the benefits he derived from committing the offense. The position taken is reparative— the service work should be in proportion to the deficit created in the community by the offense. Unfortunately, no attempt was made to articulate the size of this deficit or equate it with the type or amount of service work (if such an equation is possible). Even though no one advocated a retributive stance overtly, simple and poorly reasoned assignments of hours must appear to offenders as, at minimum, arbitrary, and more than likely, punitive.

This dialogue thus touched on some fundamental issues confronting the boards. How should they adjudicate disagreements among themselves? What is the purpose of the boards? What is community justice, and are board members' personal philosophies in conflict with this new justice philosophy? I take an optimistic view of this particular discussion. It was thoughtful and engaging as well as highly civil. Such disagreement is desirable because board members do need to sort out their own beliefs and come to, at least, a working consensus. Moreover, it is possible to conduct such explorations while conducting a hearing, keeping the discussion organized around practicalities (such as the number of hours to assign). There are risks, however. We would want to look for more involvement by the offender in these discussions. Such involvement is likely to invest the offender in the outcome rather than undermine the credibility of the board.

Conclusion

The four issues examined in this case study illustrate the rich interactional dynamics that occur when community members meet with criminal offenders in a justice process. They are rich because when a social norm is violated, community members feel compelled to mend the social fabric. How this is done, of course, varies widely, and Vermont Corrections has encouraged a particular focus that is based on restoration. Along the way, reparative boards try to establish common ground by finding points of connection between themselves and offenders. In effect, the offenders' social status within the community is in jeopardy. Their criminal actions have demonstrated an antisocial position, and community members must question offenders' ongoing intentions. A search for common ground is one strategy to lessen this uncertainty. This strategy may reduce the social distance that would otherwise outcast offenders. Instead, it allows for their reintegration and renewed membership in the community.

Norm affirmation processes also speak to the uncertainty that community members feel about offenders. They are also concerned with how the offense creates a more general uncertainty about the status of the community's moral order. Affirmations of local norms by board members in concert with offenders help remind all present of the need communities have for social control. In this sense, norm affirmations are a kind of moral education.

One of the biggest challenges to a successful board hearing is offender resistance to engaging in the process, particularly when they deny responsibility for the offense. These hearings are neither diversions nor dispute resolution processes; the offender has been found guilty in court. Nevertheless, offenders have an incentive to minimize their burden of responsibility, both psychologically and materially. They may very well have convinced themselves that no harm was done or the act was no fault of their own. Board members then face the task of disclosing the harm and getting offenders to acknowledge their role.

Finally, we have seen that board members sometimes disagree among themselves. This is expected, of course, in any group decision-making process. But it is exacerbated by virtue of the novelty of the boards and ambiguity in our culture's definition of criminal justice. We often seek multiple goals, and sometimes these are not compatible. I have observed boards that manage disagreement in a variety of ways: by ignoring it, by holding a recess so the offender will not observe it, and, as I illustrated above, by engaging in civil debate with the offender present.

Clearly, the four issues examined here deserve more sustained examination. And clearly, many other issues figure prominently in the offender/community relationship. I have referred several times to the work of Erving Goffman (1967). Another of his insights is that individuals are continuously engaged in "face work," or actions that save face or protect oneself from the critical judgments of others. This is true, he claimed, of all human encounters, let alone ones in which transgressions are the major focus.

> Much of the activity occurring during an encounter can be understood as an effort on everyone's part to get through the occasion and all the unanticipated and unintentional events that can cast participants in an undesirable light, without disrupting the relationships of the participants. (p. 41)

Board hearings are anxiety-provoking encounters, and everyone involved works hard to get through the occasion without disaster. The classic means to "get through" is avoidance of the tense subject. But the boards are charged with addressing the offense head on, without minimizing it (or exaggerating it). They must talk about exactly that which everyone would like to ignore and wish never happened. Moreover, they are asked to accomplish two difficult tasks: they must try (1) to resolve the injustice by getting the offender to agree with reparations and (2) to elicit the offender's commitment not through coercion but by reintegrating the offender into the role of socially responsible community member. When they accomplish these tasks, the reparative boards will have succeeded not simply in surviving a difficult encounter but in realizing a new conception of criminal justice based on the community justice ideal.

Notes

1. These five goals are a recent revision of an original set of four offender contract goals: (1) to restore and make whole the victim(s) of the crime, (2) to make amends to the community, (3) to learn about the impact of the crime on victim(s), and (4) to learn ways to avoid reoffending in the future.

2. Judges often impose additional conditions that go beyond the scope of the boards. Boards, for example, are not empowered to suspend licenses or impose other restrictive conditions. The extent to which judges' conditions are consistent with the board's restorative justice focus is an important matter for inquiry.

3. In one case that I observed but did not videotape, an offender agreed to pay an additional amount of restitution to that which was ordered by the court (based on what the victim reported during the hearing). Yet minutes after the meeting, the offender told her probation officer that she believed the addition was unfair but was too afraid to speak up during the hearing. The probation officer brought her back before the board to address this, where she immediately acquiesced once again.

References

Associated Press. 1993. "Protests Force Sex Offender to Move From Second Town." *New York Times*, July 20, p. A8.

Clear, Todd R. and David R. Karp. 1999. *The Community Justice Ideal*. New York: Westview.

Dooley, Michael. 1995 Annual Issue. "Restorative Justice in Vermont: A Work in Progress." *Topics in Community Corrections* 31-6.

Finn, Peter. 1997. *Sex Offender Community Notification*. Washington, DC: National Institute of Justice.

Goffman, Erving. 1963. *Stigma: Notes on the Management of Spoiled Identity*. Englewood Cliffs, NJ: Prentice-Hall.

——. 1967. *Interaction Ritual*. Garden City, NY: Anchor.

Hudson, Joe, Allison Morris, Gabrielle Maxwell, and Burt Galaway. 1996. *Family Group Conferences*. Monsey, NY: Criminal Justice Press.

John Doble Research Associates, Inc. 1994. *Crime and Corrections: The Views of the People of Vermont*. Report to the Vermont Department of Corrections, Waterbury, VT.

Karp, David R. and Todd R. Clear. 2000. "Community Justice: A Conceptual Framework." Pp. 323-368 in *Criminal Justice 2000*, vol. 2 in *Boundaries Changes in Criminal Justice Organizations*. Washington, DC: National Institute of Justice. Retrieved October 6, 2000 (www.ojp.usdoj.gov/nij/criminal_justice2000/vol2_2000.html).

Karp, David R. and Lynne Walther. 2001. "Community Reparative Boards in Vermont." Pp. 199-218 in *Restorative Community Justice: Cultivating Common Ground for Victims, Communities, and Offenders*, edited by Gordon Bazemore and Mara Schiff. Cincinnati, OH: Anderson.

Perry, John G. and John F. Gorczyk. 1997. "Restructuring Corrections: Using Market Research in Vermont." *Corrections Management Quarterly* 1:26-35.

Umbreit, Mark S. 1994. *Victim Meets Offender: The Impact of Restorative Justice and Mediation*. Monsey, NY: Criminal Justice Press.

Vermont Department of Corrections. 1998. *FY1997 Facts and Figures*. Waterbury, VT: Author.

The following case study is bittersweet. When we first discovered the Southside Restorative Justice Project of the Tallahassee Neighborhood Justice Center in Florida, we believed it to be a program full of promise and an excellent example of restorative community justice. When we asked Evelyn and Joanna to write this case study, the program was flourishing. By the time they completed the chapter, the program was dismantled (although there is current planning for revitalization). What we see in this case study is the challenge, sometimes insurmountable, of bringing theory into practice. We learn about the obstacles to implementation as well as the creative ideas that inspired the program.

Two ideas are central to this case study: restorative justice and the community justice center. The relationship between restorative justice, generally defined as an approach to justice that focuses on the repair of the harm of crime, and community justice is an important issue. In our minds, community justice is not possible without restorative justice, and restorative justice is not possible without the active participation of the community.

Restorative justice is often contrasted with retributive justice. Both are primarily "backward-looking" sanctioning theories—that is, focused on holding offenders accountable for their past behavior, rather than focused on preventing future offending. (Deterrence, incapacitation, and rehabilitation are "forward-looking" punishment philosophies.) Retribution holds offenders accountable for their past behavior by providing a punishment that approximates the pain they inflicted on victims and the community. By punishing the offender, the society expresses its moral outrage and defines clearly the moral order—what is acceptable and unacceptable behavior of its citizenry. In contrast, restorative justice holds offenders accountable by requiring that they make amends to victims and the community. Instead of the state denigrating the offender, the offender restores and repairs. Instead of obligation defined as the suffering of pain in response to pain caused, it is defined as the effort to "make right the wrong." The Southside Restorative Justice Project employed this concept by bringing community volunteers together with juvenile offenders to create restorative contracts.

In the last chapter, we focused on the Vermont Community Reparative Boards, a probation program managed by the Vermont Department of Corrections. In practice, the Southside Restorative Justice Project operates similarly to the Vermont boards. Yet, our central concern in that chapter was the dynamic role of citizen volunteers as they work with offenders, not the restorative justice agenda. This chapter fully examines the restorative justice idea.

Another important comparison between the Vermont boards and the Tallahassee project is the role of community justice centers. Community justice centers are a new idea (although they have some roots in the neighborhood justice centers of the 1970s and community mediation centers). One of the astonishing outcomes of the Vermont probation program has been the creation of several community justice centers—in Burlington, Bennington, St. Johnsbury, and more are on the horizon. Community justice centers mark the transition of justice practices away from propriety control of the criminal justice system and their return to the community. The centers in Vermont are a direct result of citizen participation in the Reparative Probation Program. Excited by their opportunity to play a meaningful role in the justice process, volunteers began to explore other opportunities for participation. Community justice centers were created to provide educational resources to the local community about justice practices, house public meetings regarding criminal justice issues, and centralize local volunteer efforts for crime prevention and criminal justice activities.

In Tallahassee, the line of causation was just the reverse. The Tallahassee Neighborhood Justice Center was created first and sponsored a number of different activities, though none of them focused on restorative responses to crime problems. As the Center grew, it saw the need for a restorative justice program and created the Southside Project. Ultimately, the community justice center may become the central feature of community corrections, a true partnership between the community and the criminal justice system in the service of crime prevention and just responses to offenders in the community.

Chapter Four

Restorative Justice, Reparation, and the Southside Project

Evelyn Zellerer
Joanna B. Cannon

The current criminal justice system, both in its policies and practices, focuses on the offender as a lawbreaker. Crime is reduced to legal questions of guilt and punishment. Mounting evidence, however, is indicting the justice system itself for its failure to resolve crime and address the needs of victims and communities. The judicial system has typically only done more of the same—"get tough" and tougher on offenders, especially through the increased use of incarceration. Yet, fear of crime and dissatisfaction with outcomes remain high. The justice system is currently in a state of crisis, and nowhere is this crisis more evident than in the United States.

In the last century, we have limited the debate and practice of criminal justice to either retribution or rehabilitation (or some combination of both). However, retribution, incapacitation, and rehabilitation have not, and indeed cannot, solve the crisis, "because a major cause of the crisis is the way we think about criminal justice" (Van Ness and Strong 1997:13).

Political calls for retribution can no longer be justified as providing what the "public" wants. For example, research in Vermont found that the public wants (a) safety from violent offenders, (b) treatment for violent offenders while in prison, (c) nonviolent offenders to be kept in the community but held accountable and made to repair the damage they have done, and finally, (d) to participate in the justice system (Walther and Perry 1998).

Community and restorative justice provides a third viable option that fundamentally changes our way of thinking about crime and our practice of justice. It is important to note that although a new global movement has begun, community and restorative justice are themselves not new. Various aspects of these approaches are seen in early legal systems that formed the foundation of Western judicature, ancient Hebrew justice, precolonial African societies, and indigenous justice (Galaway and Hudson 1996; Van Ness and Strong 1997:6-9; Weitekamp 1999).

It should also be noted that the terminology used and definitions of various terms continue to evolve and be debated. The two most prominent terms have become *community justice* and *restorative justice*. Although sometimes used interchangeably, they are, in fact, distinguishable (see, for example, Pranis 1998). Most important, community justice may or may not follow restorative values and principles. One of the four central dimensions of the community justice model advocated in this book is restorative justice (Karp et al. this volume).

Restoration, in theory and practice, is the focus of this chapter. We will present preliminary findings from an evaluation of the Southside Restorative Justice Project in Tallahassee. Between 1999 and 2001, data were collected from interviews, focus groups, surveys, participant observation, and case file analysis. We gathered the perspectives of program staff, criminal justice personnel, community members, as well as offenders and their parents who went through the restorative program. This research will provide insight into how the community justice model can be implemented and the numerous challenges that arise when trying to turn the vision into reality. Prior to presenting preliminary results from the Southside Project, we will begin with a discussion of what restorative justice and reparation mean.

Restorative Justice and Reparation

Restorative justice does not refer to a program but rather can be described as a "lens" (Zehr 1990). Through this lens, we look at crime and justice in a new, restorative way and use the following principles to guide policy and programs (Zehr and Mika 1997):

- Crime is a violation of people and interpersonal relationships

- Violations create obligations and liabilities

- Justice seeks to heal and put right the wrongs

Restorative justice begins with the fact that crime causes harm. It causes harm to people (the real victims, as opposed to an esoteric notion of "the state") and to relationships. Therefore, there is an obligation to repair the harm caused by an offender's behavior, to "make things right." Bazemore and Walgrave (1999) define restorative justice as "every action that is primarily oriented toward doing justice by repairing the harm that has been caused by a crime" (p. 48). All the key parties affected by crime—the victim, offender, community, and possibly also government—actively participate in finding reparative solutions. As Zehr (1990) states, three primary questions arise from restorative justice: "What is the harm?" "What needs to be done to make it right?" and "Who is responsible?"

Our attention, therefore, is directed to addressing the needs of victims, holding offenders accountable, and providing opportunities for and ensuring that there is reparation. We also discuss a problem-solving approach undertaken by the key stakeholders, in which the underlying causes of crime are acknowledged and the likelihood of future offending is reduced. Community safety is also a priority, so the seriousness of the crime and the risks posed by the offender are considered. Although the use of incarceration should be limited, certain offenders will require secure custody when they pose too great a threat to the safety of others to remain in the community. Restorative values can, nonetheless, be applied in any setting, including prison.

When a crime occurs, there are potentially many different kinds of harm as well as potentially different injured parties. The harm resulting from victimization can include financial losses, emotional or psychological effects (such as guilt, self-blame, fear, alienation), relational and social problems, and physical injury (see, for example, Elias 1986). There are, therefore, a number of dimensions of victim restoration. Braithwaite (1996) provides the following list of some of the dimensions that may require restoring: property loss, injury, sense of security, dignity, sense of empowerment, deliberate democracy, harmony based on a feeling that justice has been done, and social support.

Crime harms individual victims, the community, and possibly even the offender (Braithwaite 1996; Van Ness and Strong 1997). The harm may be done to a primary victim of a crime or to secondary victims such as family members or both. Although offenders must be held responsible and accountable for their behavior, this does not preclude also addressing their injuries (either those resulting from the crime or those that contributed to the commission of the crime). For example, an offender may also be a victim of child abuse or of racism.

Restorative advocates agree that individuals directly victimized by a crime clearly suffer injuries or losses, so these victims must be at the center of restorative responses. Most scholars also call for reparation of victimized communities; "an offense is a threat to the peace and quality of life in a community" (Walgrave 1999:139). Various issues are raised in defining *community* and articulating the nature of the harm. These issues and other debates, such as whether we should consider general society as also a victim of crime, remain unresolved (Bazemore and Walgrave 1999). There is consensus, however, on the need to consider the harms left in the wake of crime and to construct appropriate responses that aim for maximal reparation and healing.

Van Ness and Strong (1997) refer to Webster's dictionary's definition of reparation: "the act of making amends, offering expiation, or giving satisfaction for a wrong or injury; something done or given as amends or satisfaction" (p. 91). Numerous ways exist to make amends and ideally restore victims and communities. Restoration is a process as well as an outcome (Schiff 1999).

Restorative process and restorative outcomes are intimately connected, and both are used to achieve the goals of offender accountability, victim/community reparation, and community safety. Examples of restorative processes include, but are not limited to, victim-offender mediation, family group conferences, circle sentencing, and community sanctioning boards. An important principle of restorative justice that guides such processes is that all human beings have dignity and worth. "Actual outcomes will be determined by the quality of the process—not just what gets done, but how it is done" (Balanced and Restorative Justice Project 1998:51).

Restorative justice calls for creative, flexible sanctions that are tailored to the particular crime and meet the needs of the individuals involved in each case. Examples of restorative actions include, but are certainly not limited to, compensation, services for victims, and apologies. Actions may be direct, indirect, concrete, symbolic, or all four. Participation may be completely voluntary, or sanctions may involve a coercive element by their virtue of being imposed by a legal authority. Victims and offenders may meet face to face or not at all. Alternatively, victims may be represented by a surrogate victim (an individual who was not victimized by the particular offender in the case but who had previously been victimized, someone intimately close to the victim, or a victim advocate working with the actual victim). As Bazemore and Walgrave (1999) explain, "Sanctions are 'restorative' to the extent that they are carried out with the intent to repair harm, and in such a way that they maximize the likelihood of repair and satisfaction to victims and communities" (p. 51; see also Bazemore and Umbreit 1995).

Two prominent sanctions are restitution and community service (see Bazemore and Maloney 1994; Pranis 1998; Schiff 1999; Van Ness and Strong 1997; Walgrave 1999). These were developed within the traditional justice system and do not, in and of themselves, guarantee restorative aims and values. However, they both hold potential for reparation. It must be remembered that the goal is to repair harm so offenders, in being held accountable, must see a connection between their sanctions and the specific harms they caused. Walgrave (1999) thus defines community service as "unpaid work done by the offender for the benefit of a community or its institutions meant as compensation for the harm caused by an offense. . . . The compensation may only have a symbolic aspect, but it is no less important for that. The community itself is restored through the material results of the service rendered and through the peace-restoring gesture of the offender" (p. 139). A variety of innovative projects could be done, as shown in Deschutes County, Oregon, such as building a child abuse center, transitional housing shelter, park, or Habitat for Humanity house (Maloney 1998).

Offender accountability, therefore, is when wrongdoers take responsibility for their behavior and take action to repair the harm done. According to the Balanced and Restorative Justice Project (1998), taking responsibility requires

- Understanding how that behavior affected other human beings (not just the courts or officials)

- Acknowledging that the behavior resulted from a choice that could have been made differently

- Acknowledging to all affected that the behavior was harmful to others

- Taking action to repair the harm where possible

- Making changes necessary to avoid such behavior in the future (p. 9)

Requiring reparation means that we must also ensure that it is feasible and actually completed. Resources for communities and support systems for offenders must be provided. "Support without accountability leads to moral weakness. Accountability without support is a form of cruelty" (Basler 1996:47). Often offenders do not have the financial means to repay victims for their losses. Offenders could nonetheless make reparation through, for example, their labor. A centralized fund could be set up that victims can draw from and offenders contribute to (Van Ness and Strong 1997). Interagency cooperation and the utilization of community resources are necessary ingredients for addressing an offender's ability to provide reparation.

At this early stage in the development of restorative justice, "the discussion of how to achieve restoration is in its infancy" (Bazemore and Walgrave 1999:52). Given that our society is full of deep injustices, detrimental imbalances, and dominations, the practical task of restoration and justice is a profoundly challenging one. Braithwaite and Parker (1999:106) illustrate with an example: If a woman steals bread from a rich man to feed her children, the injustice of hungry children must be considered rather than simply making her pay for the bread and "restoring" harmony between victim and offender. Although structural injustices such as hunger cannot be resolved by restorative justice alone, we agree with Braithwaite and Parker (1999), who ask two things of restorative justice:

> First, it must not make structural injustice worse. . . . We should hope from restorative justice for micro-measures to ameliorate macro-injustice where this is possible (for example, finding a home for the homeless offender). Second, restorative justice should restore harmony with a remedy grounded in dialogue that takes account of underlying injustices. . . . Justice is what secures freedom as non-domination. (pp. 108-9)

As shown in this brief overview of restorative justice theory, reparation is a process as well as an outcome. Restorative justice addresses the injustices of crime, primary of which is the harm suffered by victims and communities. In the process of doing justice, offenders are held accountable, the needs of victims are met, and community safety is enhanced. These are accomplished through partnerships in which victims, offenders, and communities are respected participants. In the remainder of this chapter, we further examine restorative justice through a case example of a project in northern Florida that used community sanctioning panels for juvenile offenders.

The Southside Restorative Justice Project

As previously mentioned, the criminal justice system is in a state of crisis, and those working within this system are well aware of the problems. Therefore, community justice initiatives have not only been developed by outside scholars but also by justice officials. In Tallahassee, Chief Judge Padovano is credited with initiating and spearheading a process that led to the creation of the Neighborhood Justice Center (hereafter the Center). After only nine months of planning meetings, the doors to this court initiative opened in 1995. Located in an old railroad station in the south of Tallahassee, the Center grew to offer a variety of services, including victim-offender mediation, free legal assistance, a school peer program, internships, study circles/race relations dialogues, a support group for adult male offenders in a local correctional facility, and ultimately, a restorative justice program.[1]

The creation of a restorative justice program was a challenging one. The Center's original executive director was introduced to restorative justice through conferences and courses. After two years of education and training, including a visit by nationally recognized expert Gordon Bazemore,[2] the Center gained the support of major stakeholders and embraced restorative justice as an alternative approach to confront crime. In 1998, the Office of Juvenile Justice and Delinquency Prevention recognized the Center as the 10th National Balanced and Restorative Justice Site.

At this time, Dale Landry was hired by the Center to be its coordinator for balanced and restorative justice. Restorative justice provided a vision for the future of justice in Tallahassee. When Landry was hired, certain events had occurred within the community that added to the necessity for such an alternative approach to crime. There is clearly an overrepresentation of minorities within the justice system, and members of the lower socioeconomic, African American community felt they were being discriminated against by the system. For example, a black resident had been shot and killed by police. An investigation found that it was justified. The community, however, questioned the use of force and compared the outcome of this to another similar incident involving a white individual in a more affluent community that did not invoke a fatal response.

The community asked, is it "justice" or "just us"? Therefore, Landry felt that the time was right for implementing a restorative approach because "there was clearly a bridge that had slowly but surely been broken between the community, especially as I keep saying the lower socioeconomic community, and the system." He began by talking to representatives of the community and criminal justice agencies about building this bridge via restorative principles such as repairing the harm, increasing public safety, and building community capacity to solve problems.

At the end of 1998, the Center was awarded a two-year grant to develop a restorative justice project for youth.[3] For a number of reasons, it was decided that the project would serve the Southside community in Tallahassee. This is a large and diverse area, geographically contained by two zip codes. Its population is comprised of approximately 50/50 minority and white residents and is economically diverse, with housing projects and a country club located within the community's boundaries. Most important, Southside contains two of the city's highest crime districts, and service to a high-crime community was one of the grantors' requirements.

Although agreeing that the Southside could certainly benefit from a restorative initiative, a community member pointed out a potential unintended consequence of working in poor, minority communities: contributing to existing stereotypes. If one takes official crime statistics to decide where to start, this in itself may be perceived as racist, because it will bring you to a poor or minority population or both. The institutional funding body may not be committed to making substantial changes to how it responds to this population and to the disempowered community. Will the resources be directed to truly making a difference to how we respond to crime and create justice? The community member argued that we must be aware of and struggle with such issues but agreed that "we must attempt to strengthen, as Charlie Brown says, the weakest team in the NBA because that will strengthen the whole league." The integrity of an initiative depends on the individuals creating and implementing it.

Landry was faced with the challenge of turning restorative principles into practice. A number of individuals and groups provided guidance to the project. Three advisory groups were formed: a Criminal Justice Advisory Group, which had been providing input into the Center; a Victim Advisory Group; and Wisdom, an elder's group.

The Southside Restorative Justice Project (hereafter Project) became a community-based, restorative diversion program for juvenile offenders. The target population was youth 17 years old or younger who were charged with misdemeanors or nonviolent felonies and who resided in the two zip codes comprising Southside. Youth were referred to the program either judicially by the juvenile court judge or nonjudicially by the state attorney's office. These youth then came before a community sanctioning panel.

Community Sanctioning Panels

At the heart of this restorative initiative was the development of community sanctioning panels. The first step was to establish a committee that was comprised of community residents, the faith community, businesses, government representatives, and other interested individuals. All participation was voluntary, with no monetary compensation. These individuals underwent training in the Project and restorative justice. This committee formed the pool of candidates who served as panel members for the sanctioning of juvenile offenders.

Initially, the only requirement to join the committee or serve as a panelist was that one must live or work in Southside; however, the Project eventually allowed some individuals to serve as panelists who did not meet those requirements but who were concerned about youth in the community and interested in the Project. Landry, when asked if ex-prisoners could sit on the committee and panels, replied, "by all means." Not only do they potentially have much to offer but also much to gain. "The majority of them have families and the majority do not want to see their own children go the same route as they've gone." Offenders are also community members, and as each member becomes more involved, the community as a whole potentially becomes stronger and more empowered.

This issue is all the more important in minority communities, where so many members have been incarcerated. African Americans, particularly professionals working in the community, expressed an interest in becoming involved as volunteers. They were all too aware of the overrepresentation of their children in the criminal justice system. As Landry pointed out, "We have already lost two generations of the black community to the penal system. By the year 2001 we expect it to be over 1 million African American males in prison. . . . It was very easy for them to start buying this because the initiative was their kids."

A panel was formed on a case-by-case basis. Each panel was comprised of four to six community members and one Project staff person. Often a member of the faith community would also be present. The staff member ensured that appropriate sanctions were recommended, and the member of the faith community assisted in the peaceful resolution of cases.

Typically, a juvenile who was arrested was sent to the Juvenile Assessment Receiving Center (JARC), where cases were screened. If the youth lived in Southside, then JARC determined if their charges were appropriate for possible referral. If they were, then the appropriate information was faxed to the Project, and a file was created. The case was then sent to the state attorney's office. Either the state attorney or judge would then refer cases to the Project.

Once referred, an intake interview was conducted by Project staff with offenders and their parent or guardian. To participate in the program, a parent or guardian must accompany the youth to this interview as well as to the panel. In addition, the youth must admit guilt and agree to go through the restorative justice process.

A panelist described the panel process as follows. Panelists are first given background information, including the arrest record, of the youth. A list of questions is provided as a guide or means to get panelists thinking about what they may want to find out about. The youth then enters with one or both parents or guardians, and the panel asks questions. The youth leaves the room so the panel can talk to the parent(s) alone. The panel is not permitted to speak to the youth alone. Once questioning is complete, the panel privately discusses sanctions. After a consensus is reached, the youth and parent(s) return for the recommendations. The offender must agree to complete the sanctions within six months. The agreement is then immediately typed so everyone involved can sign it.

In one of the first cases to come before a community panel, a girl was charged with battery against her teacher. During the questioning period, the panel learned that the girl had an interest in basketball but did not know very much about it, nor did she know much about her own family. The following were the sanctions imposed by the panel:

- Participation in victim-offender mediation with her teacher (who willingly agreed)
- Apology to the teacher in front of the class (with appropriate attitude and attire)
- Two written reports and one oral presentation on two books about women WNBA basketball players (she had to locate these at a library)
- A family tree going back three generations
- 80 community service hours: 20 hours each at a library, recreational center for children's basketball, senior center, and homeless shelter
- A tour of the Juvenile Detention Center

Apparently, the mother in attendance hugged each panelist for being so caring. The teacher and principal of the school were also happy as well as pleasantly surprised with the sanctions.

Apologies, in the form of letters, essays, or verbal expressions, were frequently used as sanctions. Panels decided which form of apology would be the most appropriate for each case. Apologies were made to individual victims and to community businesses. For example, one youth was apprehended for shoplifting at Dillard's, a local department store, and wrote the manager an apology letter as one of his sanctions. Generally, apology sentiments, no matter which form, were to include statements expressing realization of the harm caused by a crime, acceptance of responsibility, and remorse for the action(s).

Community service hours were also typically included as a sanction in the hopes of positively affecting the offender and victim as well as the broader community. All parties could participate in determining a location where community service would be completed. One panelist noted, "One good thing is it takes it out of the court system and puts it in the people's hands. When this guy goes back and says 'I got 40 hours community service work,' he can't say, 'Well that SOB white judge up there.' . . . He's going to have to say it was three panelists . . . that live right down the street from me."

The panelists were given a framework to help them decide on the sanctions. They were told that the average sentence for a juvenile offender involves 40 hours of community service. However, the panelists were left to their imagination and creativity to make sanctions that were reflective of restorative principles and tailored to the offenders and their particular circumstances. For example, in one case, the juvenile offender had dropped out of school, so one sanction required that she return to high school or enroll in GED classes. The youth had expressed an interest in children, so they also recommended 20 hours of community service at a day care center in addition to 20 hours at either the library or media center, all of which were located at the school where she could enroll in classes. Because she did not have transportation, they had taken into consideration the location of the facility where she would fulfill the sanctions, ensuring that it was close to her home.

As discussed earlier, restorative goals include offender accountability and the prevention of reoffending. A panelist said the panels hoped to "make them realize that they don't want to do this again, that it's not worth their time." However, as the community justice model shows, the central focus of community justice includes reparation and reintegration, both of which were considered by panelists.

The panelists took their positions and responsibilities very seriously. They showed compassion and caring and a desire to understand the causes of crime. One common concern expressed by panelists was that parents of the offending youth often seemed to be lacking in parenting skills. One panelist stated that she wanted to sit down with the youth and tell them that the way their parents were living and the lessons their parents were teaching them were "not the way it is supposed to be!" Staff members listened to such concerns, and during the early summer of 2000, the Center and the Project created family empowerment classes that could be used as a sanction. One segment of these classes was parenting skills. Panelists used this sanction and strongly encouraged parents to attend the classes, which they usually did.

After one particular session, in which it was apparent that the parents were having difficulty with their role, a panelist with a background in social work and psychology offered to meet with the parents at a convenient location to discuss developing better parenting skills. It was obviously not an imposed sanction but was a service generously offered by the panelist, which was accepted by the parents.

Such examples coincide with the community justice model. Reparation includes the identification of tasks to be completed but also the facilitation of their completion. The sanctioning panel, and more important, the broader community, has an obligation to assist in the restoration of both victims and offenders. A variety of forms of assistance exist, such as help in finding employment. Landry, for example, spoke to businesses about potentially supporting offenders. A victim advocate argued that sincere commitment from community members is required to ensure that the initiative will be successful; people must be willing to "get in the dirt, to get up close and personal with the victim and the offender and to get to know these people."

Numerous resources are present in any community to aid in reparation, including individuals with a wealth of knowledge and entities such as schools that are very supportive of the initiative. There is much potential for community members and agencies to become involved in offenders' lives as role models and mentors as well as sources of additional services for both victims and offenders. A judge noted that there are many "wonderful people in the community who otherwise would . . . not be involved in these children's lives and probably would not have any input in how these kids are molded. And, of course, how kids are molded determines what kind of adult they're going to be and so having that community involvement and helping these children is very positive." In turn, the restorative process leads to community building and, one would hope, an increase in community capacity to be able to solve its own problems.

Follow up was part of the job of the case coordinator. If someone did not fulfill their contract, another panel was convened to examine the situation and determine whether the case would be sent to the state attorney's office. The former executive director of the Center explained: "If you mess up, you will be facing the criminal justice system. . . . I see the court system willing to walk every step of the way with us. . . . I am really glad to be in partnership with them because it gives the Center clout. . . . If someone does not abide by something that they have agreed to then there will be enforcement. . . . With criminal cases, you have got to have a backup piece."

The Role of Victims

Victims and their advocates have long struggled to gain a voice within the justice system. Their fight for recognition of their rights and needs continues. A judge pointed out that a crime in mainstream justice is considered an act against "the state," which means victims are excluded. Although there has certainly been progress in the treatment and recognition of victims, they are not truly a respected part of the process. A judge admitted that when a case comes to court, victims have a right to be heard, but their role is very limited: "I decide what justice is and very rarely do I hear from a victim as to what justice should be. . . . I'm going to make a decision based on the law and the facts. There's no real appreciation for how it directly affects the victim." A victim advocate referred to the court system as a battlefield with land mines, and said that often "victims get blown to smithereens without anybody acknowledging it."

As explained earlier, victims, offenders, and communities are the three central parties in restorative justice. Crime and justice are humanized when faces are put to all the actors and they are empowered to participate in the resolution process. Part of this process enables victims to express and offenders to understand the harm done by criminal acts (for a review, see Immarigeon 1999). It can be a powerful avenue for healing if victims are able to express themselves and gain validation. It is also more powerful for offenders to hear about the consequences of their actions directly from those affected. As a community member said, "Victims bring life and breath to the issue of accountability."

Although restorative justice principles clearly include victims, this approach has not been fully embraced by victim advocates, and victim participation remains contentious. Resistance from the victims' rights movement revolves around concerns of losing what ground they have long fought for, possible revictimization, forced participation, and lack of meaningful inclusion of victims. Victims will react differently to crime, and some will and others will not want to be involved in a restorative program.

The Southside Project had to be sensitive to all of these concerns and to reach out to the victim advocacy community. Personnel at the Center took training themselves and were open to learning from victims and victim advocates. Landry joined the local victims' coalition, was building a victim advisory board, and hoped to hire a victim coordinator.

Although victim advocates were included during the planning phases of the Project, one problem was that their role was not clearly defined. This continued to be a problem that plagued the Project. Advocates in the community were wary about the Southside initiative and resistant to Landry's outreach. One victim advocate recalled listening but went "kicking and screaming." She was concerned about revictimization and about whether victims would feel they were being forced to attend a program if they were told about it by an official. Landry had to convince people of the fact that at no time would victims be pressured or coerced into participation. An advocate pointed out that there had not been much training in the local advocacy field about restorative justice. Although still cautious, this advocate participated in the initiative and concluded that restorative justice is "definitely the trend for the millennium and we need to be intricately involved in every step of it."

In the Southside Project, offenders had to be willing to repair the harm done to the victim and community. Victims do not have to agree to allow the offender to participate in the program, nor do they come before the panels. They are able to pass on their input and information to a panel through the Project staff. Although the Project had planned to make contact with victims immediately after case referral, unfortunately this was never implemented.

The role of victims was predominately determined by the sanctions given by the panels. Panelists could, and did, make recommendations for offender contact with the victim or a surrogate victim. For example, sanctions included victim-offender mediation, victim awareness panels, and victim education. The Center had been providing mediation as well as victim awareness panels and education, so these were immediately available to the Southside Project. It was always entirely up to the victim, however, whether or not to participate.

Ultimately, the inclusion of victims was an area that the program never fully developed. Options for victim participation were explored, and many conversations took place between staff members about how to safely and respectfully include victims. Landry explained that the choice to physically exclude the victim at panel meetings involved consideration of potential problems such as possible revictimization due to the offender's anger. He knew victims had to be given the choice to participate in the restorative process, but he felt that in order to do so, a specific victim advocate position would have to be created and funded. Unfortunately, the resources were never allocated for such a position.

Landry is a strong believer in surrogate victims and used victim impact classes and panels to help offenders understand the consequences of their behavior. The issues they covered included sensitivity to victims and the rights and needs of offenders. A victim advocate pointed out that work needs to be done with both victims and offenders in order to reach a safe and constructive place for resolution and restoration. Victims need support to become survivors and to express themselves, including their possible anger or rage, constructively. Offenders need to be held accountable and appreciate the impact of their actions, but they do not need to be subjected to undue castigation. Both parties may have low self-esteem.

Specific concerns were raised by community panelists and Project staff. For example, the victim may be young (sometimes age 10 or 11), so they may not easily be able to articulate harm and make suggestions for reparation. There was also not always a clear victim. Cases referred to the Project often involved school fights in which two (or more) youth were involved and both parties were referred to diversion programs. Landry stated that what was most important in such cases was to attend to relationships and to strive for offender accountability. In some cases, it may be inappropriate for victims to participate in the sanctioning process, but a mediation may be a useful reparative action. Rather than simply looking at the crime committed, restorative justice reminds us that it is important to consider the individuals involved and the interpersonal relationships affected by the crime.

Obstacles

Community justice has great transformative potential for both the system and society. This may pose a threat to the traditional justice system. Institutions are inflexible and slow to change, so some officials will be resistant. A judge noted that many have "a view of the court system which is from the 50's. . . . They don't envision the idea that we can do something collectively."

Another judge recalled not initially understanding restorative principles nor seeing how, given the tenor of the times that is oriented toward harsh punishment, it could be implemented. Discussions have to take place to realize that restorative justice can transcend political ideologies. It makes sense according to many common political goals such as reducing crime, holding offenders accountable, addressing the needs of victims, and reducing financial costs.

One hurdle for the Southside initiative was the initial lack of support from the state attorney's office. State attorneys could have a tremendous amount of power to block a restorative process. Initially, cases were simply not being referred. The former executive director of the Center said the key to overcoming resistance is persistence, and "you have to find allies, people in power, who are willing to walk along with you."

The Southside Project was able to overcome this obstacle. They found allies, including judges and certain individuals in the state attorney's office, who understood and supported community justice. The assistant state attorney primarily responsible for case referrals expressed sincere interest in and support of the Project. Cases were then referred, but other issues arose such as time and paperwork. A difference between traditional and restorative justice is in not only how cases are resolved but also how quickly. The Project ideally wanted to see offenders within a week. The assistant state attorney agreed that this would increase effectiveness, but said it was an impossible goal. Due to the overwhelming workload of attorneys, they do not even look at files until right before first appearance. Cases are simply not processed quickly through the system. Another problem is in getting the different components of the system (e.g., the Department of Juvenile Justice and the court) to work cooperatively and efficiently together. Even if the state attorneys could work faster in deciding whether to refer a case, the Department of Juvenile Justice still needs to also process the youth. Yet another problem is obtaining and completing all the necessary paperwork.

Southside staff decided to do some of the paperwork themselves, which helped. Once they got an appropriate case from JARC, they obtained the necessary forms and put the file on the attorney's desk for review. The state attorney found this very beneficial.

Other officials of the justice system eventually also came on board. A juvenile judge said, "As I learn more about it, I'm making recommendations for more kids to go that route." This judge noted that colleagues also became excited about the possibilities.

Unfortunately, although the Project educated and inspired many people, it was unable to overcome all the numerous obstacles that emerged. The Project can be proud of its many successes such as the recruitment of volunteers and establishment of community sanctioning panels. However, personnel and administrative problems were not overcome. It is beyond the scope of this chapter to provide an in-depth discussion of the implementation process and the many lessons that could be learned from the mistakes made along the way. For example, a critical problem was that staff turnover was more than 100%. As staff resigned and new staff were hired, there were periods when the program was without a coordinator and full staff. This led to inconsistencies in program operations, including a lack of contact with panelists, discontinuity in the manner in which panels were conducted, and lapses in administrative duties such as case file documentation and report writing. In addition, as new staff came on board, there were differences in philosophical orientations. After fulfilling its two-year grant, the Southside Project was officially closed in February 2001.

Conclusion

Restorative community justice provides a wonderful and viable vision of justice. Implementing this vision in practice is a worthwhile and rewarding endeavor, yet it is also challenging. The Southside Project provides an example of how restorative principles and values can be realized in a community setting.

We have learned that one vital component for success is the individuals involved. Individuals who bring the ideal into practice need to have skills and training but also commitment to an ambitious task, to the community, and to the philosophy of restorative justice. A community member commented that "maybe in our lifetime or the lifetime of my two grandsons, something may happen different as long as there's an effort. And I think this movement, like other movements, will be tested by the commitment of those who are involved."

Many shared high hopes for the future of restorative justice in this community. When it was disclosed that the Southside Project would be ending, a statement we heard countless times from criminal justice personnel, community members, and clients was "What a shame, because it is a great concept." Key stakeholders, especially community members, have not given up, and a new executive director has been hired for the Neighborhood Justice Center. As this book goes to print, we learned that a meeting was held with the county commission, which indicated their support for the restorative justice approach. Stakeholders plan to renew the Southside initiative.

Many valuable lessons can be learned from the experiences of the Southside Project. We have not yet fully reaped the benefits of all the hard work done thus far, but perhaps in the near future the vision will come to fruition in Tallahassee. Indeed, restorative justice is a process as much as it is an outcome.

Notes

1.   We would like to acknowledge and give credit to the first and long-time executive director, Martha Weinstein, for her dedication and many years of hard work in establishing such a successful Center.
2.   Gordon Bazemore is a professor of criminal justice at Florida Atlantic University and codirector of the national Balanced and Restorative Justice Project.
3.   The granting agencies were two state agencies and one federal agency, with funding beginning in November 1998. The grant was monitored by the Florida Department of Juvenile Justice. The project itself was housed at the Center, but the Center, in turn, was supervised by the court administrator.

References

Balanced and Restorative Justice Project. 1998. *Guide for Implementing the Balanced and Restorative Justice Model*. Washington, DC: Office of Juvenile Justice and Delinquency Prevention, U.S. Department of Justice.

Basler, S. 1996. *The Book of Discipline of the United Methodist Church*. Nashville, TN: Methodist Publishing House.

Bazemore, Gordon and Dennis Maloney. 1994. "Rehabilitating Community Service: Toward Restorative Service in a Balanced Justice System." *Federal Probation* 58(1):24-35.

Bazemore, Gordon and Mark Umbreit. 1995. "Rethinking the Sanctioning Function in Juvenile Court: Retributive or Restorative Responses to Youth Crime." *Crime & Delinquency* 41(3):296-316.

Bazemore, Gordon and Lode Walgrave. 1999. "Restorative Juvenile Justice: In Search of Fundamentals and an Outline for Systemic Reform." Pp. 45-74 in *Restorative Juvenile Justice: Repairing the Harm of Youth Crime*, edited by G. Bazemore and L. Walgrave. Monsey, NY: Criminal Justice Press.

Braithwaite, John. 1996. "Restorative Justice and a Better Future." *Dalhousie Review* 76(1):9-32.

Braithwaite, John and Christine Parker. 1999. "Restorative Justice Is Republican Justice." Pp. 103-26 in *Restorative Juvenile Justice: Repairing the Harm of Youth Crime,*. edited by G. Bazemore and L. Walgrave. Monsey, NY: Criminal Justice Press.

Elias, Robert. 1986. *The Politics of Victimization: Victims, Victimology and Human Rights*. New York: Oxford University Press.

Galaway, Burt and Joe Hudson, eds. 1996. *Restorative Justice: International Perspectives*. Monsey, NY: Criminal Justice Press.

Immarigeon, Russ. 1999. "Restorative Justice, Juvenile Offenders and Crime Victims: A Review of the Literature." Pp. 305-25 in *Restorative Juvenile Justice: Repairing the Harm of Youth Crime*, edited by G. Bazemore and L. Walgrave. Monsey, NY: Criminal Justice Press.

Maloney, Dennis. 1998. "From Community Corrections to Community Justice." Pp. 209-14 in *Community Justice: Concepts and Strategies*. Lexington, KY: American Probation and Parole Association.

Pranis, Kay. 1998. "Promising Practices in Community Justice: Restorative Justice." Pp. 37-57 in *Community Justice: Concepts and Strategies*. Lexington, KY: American Probation and Parole Association.

Schiff, Mara. 1999. "The Impact of Restorative Interventions on Juvenile Offenders." Pp. 327-56 in *Restorative Juvenile Justice: Repairing the Harm of Youth Crime*, edited by G. Bazemore and L. Walgrave. Monsey, NY: Criminal Justice Press.

Van Ness, Daniel and Karen Heetderks Strong. 1997. *Restoring Justice*. Cincinnati, OH: Anderson Publishing.

Walgrave, Lode. 1999. "Community Service as a Cornerstone of a Systemic Restorative Response to (Juvenile) Crime." Pp. 129-54 in *Restorative Juvenile Justice: Repairing the Harm of Youth Crime*, edited by G. Bazemore and L. Walgrave. Monsey, NY: Criminal Justice Press.

Walther, Lynne and John Perry. 1998. "The Vermont Reparative Probation Program." Pp. 181-94 in *Community Justice: Concepts and Strategies*. Lexington, KY: American Probation and Parole Association.

Weitekamp, Elmar G. M. 1999. "The History of Restorative Justice." Pp. 75-102 in *Restorative Juvenile Justice: Repairing the Harm of Youth Crime*, edited by G. Bazemore and L. Walgrave. Monsey, NY: Criminal Justice Press.

Zehr, Howard. 1990. *Changing Lenses: A New Focus for Crime and Justice*. Scottsdale, PA: Herald Press.

Zehr, Howard and Harry Mika. 1997. *Fundamental Concepts of Restorative Justice*. Akron, PA: Mennonite Central Committee.

The community corrections' activity bottom line is reintegration. Innovation and change in correctional programming are important, but without some connection to an offender's reintegration, these new ideas can seem pretty empty. In Boston's Operation Night Light, reintegration of some of the most serious offenders in the community, young gang members, takes center stage as a probation objective.

We include Operation Night Light in our probation innovations for several reasons. This is a program that has achieved national attention, including a spot on television's *20/20,* and so it richly deserves our attention. It operates in some of the toughest inner-city areas in the United States, thus setting it apart from other programs set in small-town, rural, and suburban settings. It has a particular focus that is undeniably important—Night Light seeks to reduce gang violence and youthful fatalities.

This program also illustrates a point about probation innovation that often gets little attention: The innovations in the new community corrections paradigm are not soft on crime nor are they directed to only the less serious, nonviolent offender. Operation Night Light is unabashedly serious about public safety, and it works with a combination of strict accountability and multifaceted support. To be effective, a reintegration program in most urban settings must be both demanding of its clients and supportive of their lives.

Boston's strategy works for several reasons. It begins with a deep commitment to *norm affirmation* in the way that probationers are held accountable for compliance with the conditions of their probation terms. The day-and-night *offender supervision* enables the Operation Night Light staff to carry out and enforce the orders of the court, with the result that probation supervision gains in its credibility both with clients and with other agencies such as the police. The premise of the program is to disseminate a clear and unmistakable communication of what behavior will not be tolerated and what actions are to be expected.

The leaders of Boston's approach do not simply call for accountability. They are equally clear that supervision is of limited value if it does not provide the kind of *support network development* that most offenders need to become successfully reintegrated. Thus, the Operation Night Light staff work closely with family members and community groups, such as churches, to build supportive relationships within the community. The youth under supervision of the Operation Night Light staff are not expected to make it entirely on their own. They are linked to support systems that help to sustain prosocial behavior.

These support systems are augmented by an array of programs that provide an opportunity for *competency development*. Operation Night Light links its clients to training programs and treatment programs that enable clients to develop life skills for long-term social adjustment. The key idea is that former gang members cannot make the transition to reintegrated citizenship without real-life choices that help to replace what the youth got from the gang involvement. The use of programs to develop life competence is a recognition that young people who get into trouble are often deeply challenged to find the pathways out of law-breaking behavior. If community supervision is to work, it must show some of the way to these alternative life choices.

In the end, the Boston Operation Night Light program demonstrates a profound commitment to public safety in an environment in which any other priority would make little sense. The frontiers of community-based correctional activity have little future unless they address the central concern for safer streets. Yet any attempt to hold public safety as a high value runs the risk of raising anti-citizen rhetoric or making offender reintegration even harder than it is today. Operation Night Light is a lesson in how to sustain a concern for public safety that has a belief in the value of offenders and their futures as a centerpiece of the very meaning of safety.

Chapter Five

Reinventing Probation and Reducing Youth Violence

Boston's Operation Night Light

Ronald P. Corbett, Jr.

Two crises converged in the early 1990s in a way that led to historic change in important sectors of the criminal justice system. The first crisis was reflected in a heightened concern in U.S. cities about dramatically escalating rates of youth violence, particularly homicide. The second was a crisis of legitimacy besetting the practice of probation nationwide. As the end of the decade approached, remarkable progress was made on both fronts, and the stories are intertwined.

It takes a crisis to change a bureaucracy. Convulsed by dramatically rising rates of youth homicide in the early 1990s, Boston's probation and police officials threw out existing blueprints in a desperate search for more effective strategies. A fearsome necessity became the mother of reinvention.

Operation Night Light, a police-probation partnership involving intensive home and street contacts with high-risk offenders during evening hours, emerged in 1993 as a wholly new approach for combating youth violence. Night Light rested on the stunningly simple premise that "you can't fight fires from the station house" and was designed to reverse the trend of deskbound probation officers working primarily out of their offices, with little visible presence in the community, in an anemic form of community corrections disparagingly referred to as "fortress probation."

Night Light worked, particularly because it combined with several other imaginative policing, prosecutorial, and community outreach strategies. Youth homicides dropped steeply, and the city grew hopeful again.

The success of Night Light provided momentum for a thorough rethinking of probation strategies throughout Massachusetts and led to a new model that placed increased emphasis on tighter supervision and stricter enforcement, coupled with a heightened presence in the community. Officers subsequently felt a new confidence in their efforts and gained a greater respectability in the public eye.

A similar sense of renewal and reform emerged in a number of states around the United States, notably Washington, Wisconsin, Arizona, and Virginia. Probation executives from these and a few other states networked through the American Probation and Parole Association (APPA) to share information and experiences, publicize their still nascent efforts, and to enlist converts to the cause of a reinvented probation.

The next section presents an overview of one major element in Operation Night Light. In the following sections, some of the context, operations, early experiences, and eventual results of Night Light are presented. Then I identify six major lessons learned about the nature of youth violence, the strategies that seem to avail against it, and the agency, community, and political dynamics that such efforts unleash.

In the concluding section of the chapter, I offer some tips on replication, combining what may be helpful hints with important cautionary notes. Though sound and empirically tested programs can travel to other jurisdictions, their exportability can be exaggerated, because so much of what we attempt is bound by local circumstances and subcultures, defying the notion of "one size fits all" interventions. What counts is grasping the principles at work in any successful effort and customizing them to a new site rather than transplanting a program whole to an often significantly different time and place.

Operation Night Light:
History, Operations, and Impact

In the early 1990s, communities across the United States were experiencing a worrisome surge in serious violence committed by juveniles, reflected in increasing numbers of homicides committed by teenagers. In the face of this disturbing trend, these same communities searched for policies that could stem this bloody tide. The problem became more urgent in the face of predictions from Professor James Fox of Northeastern University, among others, who foresaw a major increase in juvenile violence occurring by the end of the decade, due to changing demographics (Fox 1996).

In the late winter and early spring of 1988, Boston began to experience the first effects of a developing network of rival and violent youth street gangs. Boston Public Schools' security personnel saw the emergence within the schools and documented the first list of gangs and individual gang members and the schools they attended. The list described loosely federated groups organized around very specific territory. These gangs started what has become the custom of gangs' naming themselves for the street or public housing development in which the members live.

As the police department struggled for a strategy, gang activity and its effects grew more serious. The summer brought horrific shooting incidents on the streets during daylight hours, with rival gang members gunning each other down in drive-by and ride-by shootings. In August 1988, the city's attention was riveted to a ground zero in the gang violence explosion, the intersection of Humboldt Avenue and Homestead Street in Roxbury. Twelve-year-old Darlene Tiffany Moore was shot in the head and killed by crossfire. Rival gang shooters transformed her into a "mushroom" (the gang jargon for an innocent victim) and a symbol of the horror as she sat atop a mailbox, talking with friends.

A city that experienced 75 homicides and 5,920 aggravated assaults in 1987 would see 95 homicides and 6,291 aggravated assaults by 1988 year end. Homicides would reach an all-time annual high of 152 in 1990. Aggravated assaults reached the decade-high peak of 6,960 in calendar year 1990. Eighteen of the homicide victims in 1990 were age 17 or younger (J. Jordan, personal communication, May 12, 1998). Crack cocaine arrived on the scene around this time, attracting the developing gangs to become distributors of this highly profitable product. Traffickers in semiautomatic handguns also identified a potential market and began running guns to the emerging gangs.

Gang behavior in the courthouses grew bolder in this period. Court officials describe regular disruptions in the courtrooms and corridors, intimidation of witnesses, and attempted intimidation of staff. One justice in the Dorchester District Court made headlines with a call for assigning the National Guard to secure the courthouse. Probation officers began to identify and catalogue gang colors and individual gang members and their affiliations.

Led by then-patrol chief and now Commissioner Paul Evans, the department's management searched for alternatives in the face of the growing numbers of shootings and homicides. By spring 1990, a new strategy was ready to take to the streets in the form of the new Anti-Gang Violence Unit.

A proper understanding of Night Light—and what it adds uniquely to the criminal justice arsenal—depends on placing it in the context of the traditional practices of probation. Probation is both a sentence and a status. As a sentence, it constitutes far and away the most popular option in use. Nationally, 60% of all offenders under correctional supervision are on probation (Massachusetts Institute for a New Commonwealth 1996). The corresponding percentage in Massachusetts is 69%. Offenders placed on probation are on conditional liberty, free to remain in the community, provided that they comply with any conditions of their probationary status set by the sentencing judge. Common conditions included avoiding subsequent arrests, reporting to a probation officer, not leaving the state without permission, and, commonly, paying restitution and obtaining substance abuse counseling or other relevant treatment.

For younger offenders, some judges had traditionally imposed curfews, although this practice had waned during the 1980s and early 1990s due to difficulties with enforcement. Parents were not as cooperative as they once were, probation officers became comfortable with 9-to-5 schedules, and they were also weary of returning to high crime areas in the evening.

The Genesis of Night Light

The building blocks of what would become Night Light were created with the fielding of a new gang unit within the Boston Police Department. Probation Officers Bill Stewart and Rick Skinner and Gang Unit Detective Bob Merner set the first block in place with a corridor conversation in the summer of 1990. Realizing they were watching the same youthful offenders from two different points on the perimeter of the revolving door, they and others from both agencies began to brainstorm new forms for collaboration. As Dorchester Chief Probation Officer Bernard Fitzgerald reported, "We began seeing the same Gang Unit guys in the courthouse every single day for four months."

Using the intelligence from their contacts with the Gang Unit and information developed from their interactions with gang members, probation officers began asking judges to include curfews and area restrictions in the conditions of probation. It was expected that this escalation in the intensity of supervision would lower the number of violations for new arrests as compliance with curfews and other collateral conditions of probation improved. This escalation in enforcement strategy was a product of the recognition that high-risk offenders required a short leash and would take advantage of any laxity, as well as the realization that the deterrent effect of curfews—and the associated compliance rates—would be predicated on strict enforcement.

On their own, Fitzgerald, Stewart, and Skinner began to move away from the existing model of probation by getting away from their desks in the courthouse. They began approaching probationers on the street, who all but rubbed their eyes in disbelief at the sight of their probation officers on their turf. In August 1991, Stewart wrote a memo to District Judge James Dolan, recounting his witnessing open drug dealing by one of his clients at 2:00 p.m. on a residential street in the district. Judge Dolan, an early supporter of the collaboration, became an even more determined backer of methods to ensure that probation would have teeth.

Police officers began to see probation as a powerful deterrent and began to carve out for themselves a new role in deterrence. Informal contacts continued to grow and yield results. On November 12, 1992, Night Light started—and Boston began its work toward a strategy of community corrections—when Stewart and Skinner got in the back seat of a police car with Merner and partner Bob Fratalia.

Well, I used to watch people walk out of court with probation as the end result, I said "That's b———!" But I can see now what good, supervised probation can do—it sounds corny—for the community. I've seen gangs decimated from a particular neighborhood only because of supervised curfews and area restrictions. So again, as I touched on before, I know so much more about probation as a tool.

—*Boston Police Detective*

Operations

A typical evening in Night Light includes the matching of a one- or two-person probation team with a similar team from the gang unit. The team meets at gang unit headquarters to prepare for the evening's work. The probation officers involved would have identified some 10 to 15 probationers they wanted to see that evening, concentrating on those cases thought to be active on the street at a given time or on those who have been slipping in terms of their compliance with probation conditions. Operating in an unmarked car and in plainclothes, these teams proceed to the first scheduled curfew check. The police team is responsible for safety issues and is sensitive to the manner in which the home is approached and also to exit areas, should the probationer seek to evade the contact. Once the security issues (which are not monumental in most cases) are addressed, the probation officer(s) approach the door and seek entry. Once inside the home, the contact proceeds as would any typical probationary home visit. Every effort is made to ensure that the parents and other family members are not alarmed by the presence of probation and police officers, and courtesy and a friendly manner are emphasized.

The purpose of the visit is to ascertain whether the probationer is home in observance of the curfew, to reinforce the importance of strict observance of all conditions, and to inquire of any parents present about the behavior of the probationer, both in the home and in the community. After those basic objectives are accomplished and any other issues of concern to any of the parties are addressed, the team thanks everyone for their cooperation and goes on to the next scheduled contact.

It is not uncommon for a team to stop at a park or street corner where youth are congregated to determine whether any probationers are present and also to demonstrate to the youth of the city that the probation and police departments are working together in the evening and are interested in the whereabouts and activities of young people on probation. We have learned

---

We can use Night Light to target community concerns. If we have a rash of shootings, drive-bys, drug dealing, community complaints, we can call the court, be it Roxbury or Dorchester Court, and make all our area checks down here. So besides the added uniform presence, drug unit, detectives, and everybody else from here, we have probation officers down there to start shaking everybody's tree too. If nothing else, it just defuses it.

—*Boston Police Officer*

that word spreads fast that there is a new mode of operation in probation and a new level of jeopardy for those who would ignore their probationary obligations.

Costs and Benefits of the Program

The partnership between probation and the police was sustained because both sides were reaping tangible and significant benefits. From the probation point of view, the presence of the police makes it possible to enter the most crime-ridden areas of the city into the late evening. That is, the police provide a high degree of security for probation officers who are not armed or equipped with telecommunications capacity. Also, because of the familiarity between the departments that has grown out of Night Light, there is now routine sharing of information on a citywide level regarding the identities of those on probation; any information obtained by any police officer concerning the activities of a probationer (whether the subject of Night Light or not) can be passed on to probation. Although it may seem an obvious strategy, it does not seem to be the practice in most jurisdictions to routinely exchange information between probation and law enforcement. This failure robs probation of access to the contacts and observations made by police who are working the community on a 24-hour, 7-day-per-week basis and therefore have more eyes and ears working the streets than even the most proactive probation department can muster. This increased flow of information and intelligence regarding probationer activities has been one of the greatest by-products of Night Light.

In sum, from probation's point of view, there is a new credibility to probation supervision and the enforcement of curfews and area restrictions that was not present when probation activities were limited to the 9-to-5 p.m. time frame. Feedback from offenders, police, parents, and community members alike indicate that the kids are aware that things have changed and have become more cautious, not to say more compliant, in their behavior. This is a breakthrough.

From the police perspective, they now have a tool available to them that significantly enlarges their own power. Many police officers will speak of the frustration that comes with knowing certain offenders are active in a community but being unable to control them due to the difficulties involved in crime detection and apprehension. Although not all offenders being targeted by the police are on probation, both common sense and the available data suggest that probationers account for upwards of 20% of all serious crime (Council on Crime in America 1996). Any strategy that can legally

These are a few examples that come to mind of the benefits of a strong probation enforcement policy. One of the most striking examples is that of a young man who, along with his brothers, was the leader of a very violent drug-involved gang in the Dorchester area.

His mother made a plea for him in court, to prevent him from being incarcerated. She said that if the court allowed him to continue on probation, she would keep him at her new home in Plymouth.

The young man's terms of probation were written so that he couldn't be in Dorchester at any time other than to go to court. Within the next two days, the defendant's probation officer, while riding with the gang unit, spotted the defendant in the back of a taxi. The police stopped the taxi, and when they approached it, they observed the probationer trying to hide an object, which turned out to be a nine-millimeter handgun.

He was arrested for violation of his probation and possession of a firearm. He was found in violation of probation and committed to prison.

By virtue of this action, we were able to put a bit of a block on the activities of this gang. Another example of the benefit of the Night Light program is evidenced by the young man who said that his probation officer saved his life. The young man came to his probation officer on a Monday morning and said that, had it not been for fear of being caught, he would have been with three friends who were arrested for a double murder.

He said that he had been asked to go with his friends to a party on Friday evening. He declined the invitation, citing the fact that he had curfew and his P.O. periodically checked on him at his home, and if he were out, he would be found in violation and sent to jail.

The probationer stayed home, and his friends tried to rob two young men of their jewelry at a party, and when they resisted, they shot and killed them.

The probationer said that he had no doubt that he would have been part of that had he not been afraid of violating his curfew.

> —*Bernard L. Fitzgerald, Chief Probation Officer,*
> *Dorchester District Court*

target this group through closer surveillance and supervision can have a deterrent effect. Deterrence is achieved through incapacitating probationers by requiring that they avoid certain areas and also be in their homes at a reasonable hour each evening and not on the streets at times when gang-related violence flourishes. The understanding not lost on probationers is that although they will most often not be detected undertaking criminal activity, their failure to abide by court-ordered conditions can put them in jeopardy of incarceration just as certainly as if they were arrested for a new offense. Put differently, the threshold for depriving them of their liberty is much lower than it is for the nonprobationer and permits their removal from the street for a variety of noncriminal behaviors.

The police both marvel at and appreciate the power of probation officers in this respect. Members of the gang unit have often commented on how the kids fear their "P.O." more than they fear a uniformed officer. Provided that this broader power is used fairly and judiciously, it does put a formidable crime-fighting technique on the street as a supplement to that which is achieved through conventional police strategies.

A Balanced Approach

It was understood by all participants in this new approach that more credible enforcement had to be leavened by a commitment to provide appropriate services and interventions to youth who frequently needed help and support in finding a new, prosocial direction as they abandoned the gang life. The help came in three related forms: job assistance, faith-based counseling, and personal advocacy.

Access to employment was at the top of everyone's list. Getting kids jobs served multiple purposes. Work kept youth busy and therefore unavailable for gang activities. It also provided spending money and, in other instances, basic provisions for neglected younger siblings. Finally, it was a means to instill the habits of punctuality, following direction, and interacting appropriately with peers and the public, all sorely needed by the targeted youth.

In the early 1990s, the city of Boston greatly expanded its summer jobs program, so that it was realistic for all youth who were interested to have a good chance of locating summer employment. Key officers in the gang unit contributed their own personal efforts to the cause and developed, after securing corporate support, what came to be known as the Summer of Opportunity (SOO). SOO provided youth referred by gang unit officers with a combination of work experience and life skills training. Those youth who successfully completed the summer program (which an average of 90% were able to do) were provided part-time jobs during the school year (Buntin 1998).

At-risk youth in Boston found a second stream of support coming from an entirely new direction. In May of 1992, a local Baptist church had experienced the unspeakable: a gang-related stabbing and shooting took place during a church service. In the wake of this shocking event, inner-city clergy mobilized to address the church's role in combating youthful violence. The 10 Point Coalition was formed, comprised of ministers committed to taking their message to the streets in outreach to the hardest hit areas. These initial forays into gang areas led to the slow but steady development of relationships between kids and clergy that evolved into court advocacy and church-based programming such as Gangs Anonymous meetings, sponsored and attended by church leaders (Buntin 1998).

The involvement of clergy and other church folk lent a special cast to the ongoing efforts. The 10 Point Coalition sponsored prayer meetings and special liturgies in which blessings were bestowed on those working to support at-risk youth. To many of those involved, this new and decidedly spiritual dimension was deeply felt. It was as if the Almighty was smiling on Boston's efforts and bestowing a welcome and amazing grace on the undertaking.

These efforts were rounded out by a growing corps of streetworkers, hired by the mayor, whose charge was to hit the streets and work with young people in crisis wherever and whenever they could be found. The streetworkers were hired for their skills in developing rapport with young people and mobilizing community resources. Greeted initially with suspicion by the police, in time a close, mutually respectful situation developed that allowed the police to get the message out to gang leaders without the static that came with direct communication. The streetworkers helped head off trouble when alerted to emerging beefs, worked with kids who the police or probation might identify as on the cusp of serious trouble, and connected youth with city and other services that created healthy options for them to pursue (Buntin 1998).

The incorporation of this emphasis on services, outreach, and advocacy gave needed balance to the Boston strategy and gave moral authority to the efforts of the police and probation. Both clergy and streetworkers identified themselves with the interest of community members and could not have supported a strategy that relied on stepped-up enforcement to the neglect of services and support. This commitment to a balanced approach, which had the manifest support and involvement of Boston's most aggressive police officers, made unconventional alliances possible. The lion lay down with the lamb, as it were. The youth saw a new seriousness about stemming youth violence coupled with a genuine, consistent campaign to identify and increase the help available to them. Stereotypes and rigid role definitions broke down, all in the service of saving Boston's children.

A recently published case study of the Boston strategy, developed at Harvard University's Kennedy School of Government, put the matter this way:

The outreach programs established by the Gang Unit had a two-fold effect: they benefited kids and gave the police the credibility it needed to build close ties to the 10 Point Coalition and other service organizations. The presence of these relationships in turn created a reservoir of good will that allowed the police and other law enforcement agencies to intensify their policing efforts without alienating large segments of the black community.

"If we [the 10 Point Coalition] had not played a role in the intervention and prevention process in Boston, what you would have had was something akin to apartheid," says (Reverend Jeffrey) Brown. "You'd have had the police versus the youth. It would have been Dodge City." (Buntin 1998:19)

Program Impact

What difference have the more than 6,000 Night Light contacts (home visits, street contacts, etc.) made in the last six years? Although direct impact is notoriously difficult to prove, the trends in the impacted areas, in terms of declining rates of homicide and other violent crimes, are encouraging. To point to some recent data, there was 1 juvenile homicide during 1996, 1 in 1997, and 1 through June of 1998, compared to 16 for 1993 (J. Jordan, personal communication, May 12, 1998). The data presented in Exhibits 5.1, 5.2, and 5.3 document a decline in homicides during the period in which Night Light has operated.

Although no one involved with Night Light feels this positive trend is primarily attributable to Night Light, all the staff involved believe strongly that compliance with probation as well as lessened levels of gang-related violence are at least partially attributable to the efforts of the Night Light staff. The networks that grew out of this innovation, which brought together clergy, streetworkers, community leaders, and researchers, as well as criminal justice personnel, were regularly in touch with offenders in the impacted neighborhoods and were unanimous in their perception that probationary sentences and those that enforce them were seen in an entirely new light. David Kennedy of Harvard University's John F. Kennedy School of Government commented frequently on how often gang members he spoke to felt restrained by curfew checks, area restrictions, and more frequent and unannounced home visits that came with the Night Light regimen.

In addition, court personnel believe that probationary sentences have gained a new and enhanced credibility due to the stricter enforcement of key conditions that Night Light provides. It is clear now as it has not always

Exhibit 5.1. Boston Homicides, All Ages

Year	All Homicides
1990	153
1992	76
1993	98
1994	85
1995	96
1996	61
1997	43
1998	34
1999	17

NOTE: Data for 1999 are as of July 22, 1999.

been in the past—the word is on the street, so to speak—that those on probation must take their obligations seriously or they will be detected in not doing so and consequences will ensue.

There is also the hard to measure but real reassurance that comes to those neighborhoods where Night Light takes place. The knowledge that probation officers are around with the police ensuring that probationers are off the streets in the evening brings a measure of relief to hard-hit communities. It is also very clear that the parents of these young people, who are often in a losing battle to keep their sons from responding to the lure of the streets, genuinely appreciate the support they receive through curfew enforcement. Although this program is designed primarily to deter these

Exhibit 5.2. Boston Juvenile Homicides

Year	Homicides, 16 and Under
1992	8
1993	16
1994	6
1995	4
1996	1
1997	1
1998	1

NOTE: Data for 1998 are through June 30, 1998.

Exhibit 5.3. Boston Juvenile Homicides by Firearms

Year	Homicides, 16 and Under
1992	5
1993	10
1994	5
1995	2
1996	0
1997	1
1998	1

NOTE: Data for 1998 are through June 30, 1998.

young offenders from committing any new crimes, their parents recognize that it also serves to keep these same young people from being victimized themselves in the mortal combat that envelops their streets.

The Promise of Partnership

As with any new public initiative, the accumulation of experience across multiple sites and the completion of sound evaluative research will eventually form the basis for a reliable assessment of partnerships such as Night Light. Though these partnerships are still in their infancy, nevertheless some observations can be offered on how these new alliances can help in addressing the real crisis facing contemporary probation.

First, on a very practical level, a simple but consistent exchange of information between probation and police can serve the goals of both agencies. Both systems are concerned with suppressing offenders, and that end can be well served through sharing the surveillance task so that probationers will sense the greater risk of discovery and be deterred from criminal activity. Compliance with court order conditions is also enhanced through police cooperation. For example, where convicted batterers are prohibited from approaching the residence of their victims, discovery of a violation is greatly increased when the police who patrol that area are familiar with the offenders and the prohibition. On the other side, the police are potentially aided in investigating criminal incidents by knowing local probationers and their criminal histories and soliciting probation officer assistance in identifying potential suspects.

Beyond helping probation officers strengthen their oversight of offenders, a working relationship with the police can afford an opportunity to undertake the task of apprehending absconders, traditionally neglected by many probation departments due to staff shortages, insufficient training, or the lack of appropriate equipment. Locating and arresting fugitives is second nature to law enforcement, and this expertise can be shared to the benefit of probation.

Beyond these tangible gains is the harder to measure but nonetheless real public relations payoff that can accrue from being identified with law enforcement. The same national and local polls that reflect so poorly on probation give police very high popular ratings. There is a potential coattails phenomenon here, with some of the same positive sentiment felt for the police accruing to probation officers as they take on functions more akin to law enforcement and are visible in the company of the police. To some, this may appear to be pandering; the attendant dangers are addressed in the following section. However, where the partnership serves legitimate correctional ends, no wise probation executive should fail to capitalize on the improved perception of probation that so many of the initial sites have reported (National Institute of Corrections 1997).

The Perils of Partnership

Sociologist Robert Merton was the first to introduce the concept of "unintended consequences" into policy and program analysis, and most administrators are only too familiar with its validity (Merton 1996). Initiatives undertaken with only positive intentions in mind frequently can perversely set off negative consequences that often overtake any gains.

Although it is still early in the development of these models, some potential trade-offs have already caused concerns among those close to the efforts. In general, the dangers have at least the following three manifestations: mission creep, mission distortion, and organizational lag.

Mission Creep

Because many of these partnerships are born of or connected eventually with community policing efforts, the demands on staff time and agency resources escalate as probation officers' role definition expands in a way similar to that which has occurred with "community" police officers. In the existing sites where partnerships are flourishing, participating probation officers are engaged in a variety of new, collateral activities that come under the rubric of community building but take the officers well beyond the scope of their normal duties. Acting as a broker for any human services, attending community functions, and responding to complaints unrelated to probation are a few common examples. For police officers relieved of other responsibilities or who would be otherwise conducting general patrol, this may not be burdensome. For probation officers still carrying traditional caseloads, the time conflicts are apparent and could easily compromise effectiveness. With the right organizational and structural changes, these problems can be avoided, but such changes are often unaddressed.

Mission Distortion

Despite the best efforts of administrators who anticipate the problem and work against it, there is still a real threat that partnerships with law enforcement will be perceived and understood, particularly within probation agencies, as an abandonment of the treatment mission in favor of a near-exclusive emphasis on enforcement.

Probation has always been seen as a philosophical battleground, where the "cop" and the "social worker" types fight it out for ascendancy. A move to work collaboratively with the police will almost inevitably be seen as a victory for the cops within the probation ranks; this has implications for agency morale and the relative emphasis given to functions based on the perceived reward ratios. In other words, the treatment types may go into a funk and wonder what has become of the agency they loved. Operation Night Light reaped a degree of positive publicity unparalleled in the 120-year history of the agency. It would be very tempting for any manager, seeing this public relations coup, to immediately make a police partnership a priority overriding any other concerns. In the meantime, attention to those functions identified with rehabilitative services can suffer, and observant staff can draw the obvious inferences.

The Greeks were right—balance is everything in life. But it is devilishly difficult to maintain in the face of rapid change, shifting priorities, and new trends. It is important for administrators to remember to put only some of their eggs into each new basket and to ensure that new strategies yield to rather than overtake the agency's preexisting and, one hopes, well thought-out mission statement.

Furthermore, if the research in community corrections for the last 15 years has taught us anything, it is that an exclusive or even primary emphasis on enforcement, surveillance, and control strategies in probation will not succeed. Without the array of services available through the city of Boston, the business community, and the court system—including camp scholarships, summer jobs, employment training, and substance abuse treatment—the Night Light officers would have been severely hampered in their work. Whenever a high-risk probationer showed signs of wanting to get out of the life, the supervising probation officer had options for referral that enhanced the chances for success with the case.

What was unique about Night Light was not the services provided—though they were surely critical—but the fact that, for the first time in recent memory in Boston, the offenders felt they were truly being supervised. They recognized that their actions were known to either probation or the police, who were pooling their intelligence, and that therefore their margin for error was greatly reduced. It is clear that this deterrence strategy made many more probationers amenable to going straight than was typical under previous conditions (Petersilia 1995).

Organizational Lag

Unlike the first two, the last peril is not a by-product of police-probation partnerships but rather a threat to them. The correctional landscape is littered with the remains of once promising programs that perished from lack of full institutional support. Petersilia (1998) remarks that the problem with intermediate sanctions, which she sees as having great but unfulfilled promise, is that they were never adequately supported and therefore never received a fair trial. Such has been the fate of many correctional innovations.

For probation-police partnerships to take root and flourish, they cannot simply be grafted onto existing organizational arrangements. Patterns in the assignment of work, for example, will require rethinking. Perhaps probation officers should be assigned neighborhoods instead of caseloads. Perhaps contact standards and other commonplace bureaucratic requirements should be replaced by broader, more flexible standards of practice, crediting a range of actions in the community that could deter reoffending. Management information systems may need dramatic change to attract and then reward individuals who have the qualities necessary for success in this new environment.

What is more predictable is that a new practice will be overlaid on existing customs, many of which have long since become obsolescent. Undertaking a new approach while being held to a traditional accountability structure will create real disincentives for interested staff, demoralize those who otherwise want the partnerships to succeed, and ultimately threaten the future of the program.

As with so much else in public administration, the best ideas cannot survive uninspired, timid management. True leadership, on the other hand, can make even flawed models work wonders. We shall see.

Six Lessons Learned

A man does not show his greatness by being at one extremity or another but rather by touching both at once. (Albert Camus)

1. *The Importance of Balance.* Correctional interventions must be two-fisted. An attempt to make real progress by utilizing either law enforcement strategies or treatment approaches alone is doomed to failure. The problems we address never yield to one-dimensional approaches.

Secondarily, the one-theme approach will not garner critical political support. Solutions must be bipartisan, in policy terms. The investment in enforcement clears the path for a complimentary investment in treatment. Average U.S. citizens want to see a measure of both, shifting in proportions to the realities confronted. This common sense is anything but.

2. *Publicity Builds Momentum and Commitment.* President Clinton visited Boston in February 1997 as the culmination of an extended series of positive media hits for the Boston strategy. Regular coverage by both local and national media outlets (e.g., coverage on the *ABC Evening News* in its "Solutions" series) drew popular and, more important, internal attention to the effort. Everyone wanted in—there was no lack of volunteers or resources available to support the effort.

For any new initiative to flourish, there has to be a buzz surrounding it that focuses attention and elicits support. Both an internal strategy, creating organizational incentives for involvement, and an external strategy, building political support, are critical.

Accordingly, new programs must attract the best and brightest in an agency through strong support and internal marketing by the agency's leadership and must catch the eye of key figures in the agency's authorizing environment, the circle of key public figures whose support is crucial to the agency. Nothing will accomplish this faster than sustained, positive media coverage.

3. *Nurture the Relationship Among Partners.* Partnerships of any kind are fragile affairs and require work if they are to be sustained. Regular communication and an honest effort to honor each partner's unique role and requirements are key to longevity.

In the early years of the Boston strategy, all participating agencies, including both administrative and line staff, were invited to biweekly meetings. They were well attended and served multiple functions. The frequency of the meetings allowed those present to get to know and trust each other. The opportunity to get up-to-date intelligence and to share success stories sustained interest and commitment. The open forum approach, where anyone irrespective of rank could speak to the group, made for lively meetings when the key issues surfaced.

4. *Use an Objective Outsider.* Groups, particularly if they are highly charged and successful, can develop a blindness to potential mistakes or lost opportunities. Groupthink takes over, in the flush of enthusiasm and fellow-feeling engendered by a new and exciting venture. Reality can sometimes get lost.

One antidote to this dynamic is to involve an outsider whose job, whether by design or happenstance, is to keep the project honest and aware of all developments, to look for flaws of logic, errors of omission, as well as possibilities for enhancements that only a disinterested party will easily notice.

In the Boston experience, David Kennedy played just such a role. Kennedy worked from a great respect for the practice wisdom of the participants and looked first to leverage their abilities and insights by feeding back to them in refined form the raw material of his many long and patient discussions with the key players.

Once again, an excerpt from the case study puts it best:

> Kennedy also played an important role in facilitating inter-agency cooperation. Kennedy didn't attempt to push his own approach to tackling youth violence on the group; rather, he pushed participants to think about what they could do to work more effectively together. Although many of the participants had already forged close working relationships, Kennedy's outsider perspective further encouraged working group members to drop their institutional egos. According to Kennedy, the working group process created a real sense of excitement. (Buntin 1998:25)

5. *Get Good Data.* We don't know what we don't know. Though length of experience and seeming familiarity with a problem may lull us into thinking that we understand its dimensions and true nature, gathering hard data before undertaking a new project can bring some surprises or at least impose a needed discipline on the process.

David Kennedy provided an essential service by helping the participants gather reliable data on the phenomenon and the offenders in question. Putting the up-front work into getting good data paid off in the group's understanding of the nature of youth violence. An examination of the particulars of 155 youth homicides in Boston revealed a high correlation between gang membership and gang-related activities and demonstrated the concentration of both perpetrators and victims among the relatively slim ranks of chronic offenders well known to the system. This information was critical to the development of the strategy.

Second, tracking the results of the project provided both required documentation of results to the outside world while also helping to shape and refine the emerging strategy. This is also covered in the next and final lesson.

> The country needs, and unless I mistake its temper, the country demands bold, persistent experimentation. It is common sense to take a method and try it. If it fails, admit it frankly and try another. But above all, try something. (Franklin D. Roosevelt, 1932)

6. *Be Experimental.* A bias toward experimentation is reflected in passion for novelty, flexibility, and measurability. Corrections is awash in failed strategies, and the only recourse for the prudent manager is to keep trying. Moreover, trying to find entirely new ways that break from conventional approaches is especially critical. Breakthroughs in science come from exploring new techniques for which there is often no logical support. We still don't know why some very effective medicines work. We must be similarly foolhardy in corrections. We have to love the long shot, the odd ball, the "what if" frame of mind. It is this spirit that animated the architects of the Boston strategy and accounts for much of their success.

Flexibility in design and implementation is equally important. If the ideal model cannot or does not work, modify it, tweak it, until it starts showing some results. Again, this is precisely how the most accomplished scientists work. They follow an iterative process, constantly testing, changing, and testing again. Sticking with something after it has shown flaws is not determination but stubborn pridefulness.

Finally, look for proof that you are attaining the ultimate outcomes. Have a bottom line and stay with it. In Boston, the goal always was to stop the killing. The participants never looked up until the numbers began to drop dramatically. Fewer funerals was the goal and they kept close score.

Thoughts on Replication

Principles Travel but Programs Don't

Too often, a certain model gains popularity and becomes the darling of the correctional field. Boot camps are a good, recent example. Like Cabbage Patch dolls, everyone has to have one. The trouble with adopting programs wholesale because they are in fashion and appear to work is that it ignores the reality that people, places, conditions, and resources vary significantly in ways that can both foster and impede success. What works for me will work for you only if you are just like me. Usually, you are not.

Principles can transfer, however. Looking to the essence or core properties of a program is helpful, for they can be embodied differently, depending on the key variables in the adopting jurisdiction. Custom tailor the general approach to local realities. Steal my ideas, not my programs.

It Takes a Crisis

A delegation from Boston recently visited another state interested in adopting the Boston strategy. In a meeting with the officials of that state, someone asked, "What does it take to get a program like yours started?" After a pause, I responded, "It helps if one of your churches is shot up."

The tragedy at the Morning Star Baptist Church in Boston was clearly a catalyst for much of what started in Boston. No one honestly hopes for such an event, but the cold truth is that something of that caliber is often the unplanned-for jump-start for subsequent reform. Absent a shared sense of urgency, the mandate for change is a weak and uncertain thing.

You cannot plan for and should not instigate a crisis, but you can reveal one. Sometime, seeing that there is attention drawn to otherwise little known and ominous conditions and trends can provide a critical mass of concern and coverage. A flair for the dramatic is a well-known attribute of change agents.

Look for Natural-Born Leaders

Peter Drucker, a management guru, has said that wherever something really great is happening, there is a maniac on a mission. Big results require extraordinary leaders. The best ideas in corrections are never self-executing. Uninspired management can undermine the best models, and real leadership can breathe life into the most half-baked ideas.

New projects need champions. Agencies and jurisdictions committed to radical improvements must identify and enlist talented administrators with a passion for the enterprise and a hunger to succeed. They're few in number, but every system has them. Find them and put them on the case.

Start Small

Don't launch the Normandy invasion if all you need at the moment is to take a beachhead. Overreaching squanders resources, divides attention, strains logistics, and makes retreat difficult.

Look to your most favorable circumstances and start there. Learn first what it takes to succeed. Make an early victory nearly inevitable through a concentration of force. Use that small success to build momentum. By moving slowly but consistently, you can spread yourself thick.

Take Stock of Existing Relationships

Citywide interventions require the buy-in of a diverse group of public and private officials. Historians of war tell us that soldiers risk their lives more for comrades than for cause. Social action is no different. Only hard-earned mutual trust based on personal regard will get any coalition through the inevitable setbacks.

The best working relationships don't come cheap. They are built around a lot of coffee cups, in station house back rooms, in drafty church basements, in courthouse corridors, and at the scenes of shootings. It takes a while to learn who you can rely on, whose back you are willing to cover.

Agencies wishing to take the lead in a new strategy must be assured that they have sufficient allies. If more work needs to be done on cultivating key relationships, hold off the new initiatives and build those key alliances. Your potential partners will want to know that you are dependable, honest, courageous, and a team player. Show them.

School-Probation Partnerships: The Next Frontier

Traditionally, a fire wall has existed between probation and law enforcement, impeding information sharing and collaboration. The experiences described earlier in this chapter reflect the progress that has been made in Boston (and, increasingly, elsewhere) in tearing down that fire wall, which required a redefinition of conventional roles and relationships.

Attention should now be turned to the relationship between schools and probation. Some of the same radical rethinking is needed to maximize the potential of both institutions to contribute. Recent reports (Anderson 1998) have pointed to a dearth of experimentation and creativity with respect to school-based crime prevention activities. Other recent accounts (Marans and Schaefer 1998) lament the fact that school officials and other adult authority figures in the community, including probation and police officers, too infrequently cooperate in establishing joint boundaries around and support for at-risk youth, disserving the young person, the institutions represented, and the community alike.

There are some bright spots, and these offer valuable lessons. Jeremy Travis (1998), former director of the National Institute of Justice, the research arm for the attorney general of the United States, recently reported on successful efforts at incorporating problem-solving strategies, developed first in law enforcement, to address school safety issues. Evaluative research conducted by the Police Executive Research Forum documented strikingly positive results.

Sadly, in the same speech, Travis commented on the failure of school officials and probation officials to cooperate in placing probation officers in schools, despite the overwhelming logic supporting such a strategy. Travis concludes his remarks by calling for greater partnerships between schools and key law enforcement and social service agencies.

For the last several years, Middlesex County in Massachusetts has experimented with the kinds of alliances Travis promotes and, in the process, has recast traditional roles and ways of doing business. Three particular strategies warrant mention:

1. *Community-Based Justice Meetings.* Developed originally by District Attorney Tom Reilly (now Massachusetts attorney general), each high school in the county hosts a weekly meeting involving prosecutors, police officers, probation officers, and school officials to discuss the ongoing response to at-risk youth. These meetings include the exchange of information and intelligence regarding such matters as school and community behavior and the status of any legal proceedings. In addition, the participants engage in problem solving and planning, aiming at a coordinated response to contain the youth while also providing needed services, a kind of carrot-and-stick approach. With several years of experience already, all participants laud the value of the program, and the model has been exported to all other Massachusetts counties.

2. *Project Firm.* In Framingham, one of the largest cities in the county, the school system and local probation office have collaborated for several years in a diversionary program for school offenders. When students are charged with infractions of school rules, some of which could potentially lead to a delinquency complaint, local juvenile probation officers act as hearing officers at the schools to determine if the infraction occurred and the nature of any appropriate sanctions and services. This process gets probation officers and school officials collaborating early on in the offending career of youth so that they will both understand the concern of the community for their behavior while also availing themselves of social services, if indicated. This bridge between schools and probation established through Project Firm carries over into the handling of formal delinquency complaints and spawned partnerships such as Project NIRC.

3. *Project NIRC.* Growing out of the success of Project Firm, the schools, probation, and police officials joined in a new initiative that the police dubbed NIRC (nonincident-related contact). NIRC involves joint evening patrols for at-risk students who are presenting problems in the schools or the community or both. Home contacts are made by the three representatives who educate the youth and parents on the likely consequences of further difficulty and offer services if the family is open to them. Here again, the image portrayed to the youth and the community is one of the responsible authorities in a young person's life working together to hold young people accountable and to intervene with assistance before a problem worsens.

Each of these three initiatives call on officials to act in new and unfamiliar ways, to adopt an expanded role in which they almost act interchangeably with others in the young person's life. They eliminate the fire walls referred to earlier and replace them with bridges that facilitate communication and cooperation. Each promotes what Travis believes is so urgently needed: common ownership by the key public institutions involved with youth of the need to mount a coordinated response to youthful misbehavior, leveraging and multiplying the controls and solutions that each can bring to the table in the service of community safety and individual well-being.

Albert Einstein is reputed to have said that insanity is doing the same old thing but expecting different results. Middlesex County is doing different things and getting different results and is a success story in its own right that ranks with Boston.

References

Anderson, David C. 1998. "Curriculum, Culture, and Community: The Challenge of School Violence." *Youth Violence*, edited by Michael Tonry and Mark H. Moore. Chicago and London: University of Chicago Press.

Buntin, John. 1998. *A Community Response: Boston Confronts an Upsurge of Youth Violence.* Cambridge, MA: John F. Kennedy School of Government, Presidents & Fellows.

Council on Crime in America. 1996 (January). *The State of Violent Crime in America.* Washington, DC: Author.

Fox, James Alan. 1996. *Trends in Juvenile Violence.* Washington, DC: U.S. Department of Justice.

Marans, S. and Schaefer, M. 1998. "Community Policing, Schools, and Mental Health: The Challenge of Collaboration." Pp. 312-47 in *Violence in American Schools: A New Perspective*, edited by D. Elliott, B. Hamburg, and K. Williams. Cambridge, England: Cambridge University Press.

Massachusetts Institute for a New Commonwealth. 1996. *Criminal Justice in Massachusetts: Putting Crime Control First.* October: 21.

Merton, R. K. 1996. *On Social Structure and Science.* Chicago: University of Chicago Press.

National Institute of Corrections. 1997. *Symposium on Police-Probation Partnerships*. Boston, MA.

Petersilia, J., ed. 1998. *Community Corrections: Probation, Parole and Intermediate Sanctions*. New York: Oxford University Press.

Petersilia, J. 1995. "A Crime Control Rationale for Reinvesting in Community Corrections." *Prison Journal* 75:479-96.

Travis, Jeremy. 1998. *Creating Safe Schools: Opening the Schoolhouse Doors to Research and Partnership*. Keynote Address at Conference of the Security Management Institute. New York.

Each selection in the book describes a new community justice program. But community justice is not merely a "new program." It is a new philosophy of the provision of justice services. Therein lies an important point, often not understood by the managers of community supervision agencies. Those who run community services have an understandable tendency to think in terms of new programs. This kind of thinking can become slightly faddish, and we see this in the way the field tends to bounce from one idea to another, in search of what works.

By its very nature, community justice is an idea that calls for more than mere programs, for it seeks a shift in the programmatic thinking from which any new programs might be developed. This final selection, a study of Deschutes County Community Justice in Oregon, shows how important it is to take a holistic approach to community justice innovation.

The Deschutes experience starts out with a probation department whose leaders—and later whose staff—are becoming increasingly dissatisfied with the old way of doing business. They see themselves becoming alienated from the public they are meant to serve, increasingly at odds with the clients they supervise, and asked to implement new policies in practices in which they have little confidence. The result was a turn-around in thinking that begins with the idea of community justice and ends in wholesale change in the way the probation department came to see its assignment. The scope of change is so profound that it even required a change in the name of the organization.

Deschutes County Community Justice represents the frontier in community justice in many of the ways that are now familiar to us and have been illustrated in previous chapters in this book. There is a heavy reliance upon community participation. Work with offenders emphasizes the restorative capacity of sanctions and interventions. The aim is to secure community safety through the prevention of crime and reintegration of offenders. The activities of community supervision are seen as taking place in the field, in neighborhoods, in "places," and with not just convicted offenders but also with families, neighbors, and those at risk of harm. The construction of Deschutes County Community Justice work has a distinct social justice flavor.

All of this is familiar in concept, if not typical, in how well it has been pulled off. But there is something quite extraordinary in the Deschutes experience that makes the illustration all that more compelling. The Deschutes County officials have put their money where their mouth is. They have tied community justice thinking—not just programming but an entire vision—to the way they get and spend their budget.

Working within the limitations of a traditional justice model operating at the state level, the Deschutes officials came to see that they needed to change the financial incentive structure that reinforced old practices. So they asked the state to let them keep locally all the juvenile offenders who ordinarily would be sent to state incarceration (at state expense) and then to let them also keep the state tax dollars that would have been spent on them. In effect, they said, "The crime problem in this county needs to be our problem locally. We cannot make Deschutes County better by temporarily sending our problem youth to state facilities, only to get them back later. So if the state will let us keep the money that would have been spent on those youth, we will deal with them ourselves."

That is what makes Deschutes County so important. It is a holistic community justice innovation that shows the idea at its most powerfully advanced stage.

Chapter Six

Deschutes County, Oregon

Community Justice in Action

Teri K. Martin

Etched on the façade of the Community Justice Center in Deschutes County:

Heroes are not giant statues framed against a red sky. They are people who say, "This is my community and it's my responsibility to make it better."

—Governor Tom McCall

The work we do for ourselves follows us to the grave. The work we do for our community lives on forever.

—President Theodore Roosevelt

Communities are defined not only by geography but even more by shared values and networks of relationships that encourage individual citizens to work toward the common good. Etzioni (1996:xviii) suggests that a "new golden rule should read: Respect and uphold society's moral order as you would have society respect and uphold your autonomy." The central aim of community justice is to enhance the health and safety of communities by engaging citizens in maintaining order and promoting wellness. It is a "democratic system . . . where people with the most to gain or lose accept the rights and responsibilities of collaborative decision-making" (Bucqueroux 1996:13). Community justice is a process that, at its best, is characterized by

- Active collaboration of citizens, elected officials, and public and private service agencies in *community governance*

- A focus on *preventing social problems* rather than curing them

- Recognizing and *building on community strengths and assets*

- *Involving community members in defining and resolving problems* before they escalate to crises

- *Repairing harms done* to victims of crime and their communities

- *Holding offenders accountable and improving their competency* to be productive community members

In Deschutes County, the promise and power of community justice is being realized as these principles are increasingly put into practice to create and maintain safe and healthy communities. By understanding how community justice has evolved in the unique context of Deschutes County, other jurisdictions can learn how to adapt the core principles and processes to their own local realities.

The Oregon Context

Oregon traditionally encourages the active involvement of citizens in policy making and has empowered county governments to tailor justice, health, and human service policies and practices to fit local priorities. Counties are granted the flexibility to be innovative and are challenged to demonstrate the outcomes of their efforts. But some recent policy changes pose challenges to those wishing to implement community justice.

Policies Consistent With Community Justice

Since 1974, when Oregon's legislature passed one of the first Community Corrections Acts in the United States, the state has been steadily shifting criminal justice and community corrections responsibilities and resources to its local communities. In 1995, this trend culminated in the transfer to the counties of all community corrections planning and implementation responsibilities, to be funded by the state based primarily on county population size. Local Public Safety Coordinating Councils (PSCC) were created in Deschutes County and in nearly every other Oregon county. The PSCCs bring together representatives of key criminal and juvenile justice agencies, local elected officials, and citizen activists to collaborate in developing policies and program strategies that will enhance public safety and well-being.

In 1993, following in the footsteps of Deschutes County, which created the first Commission on Children and Families (CCF), the Oregon legislature established CCFs in all other counties. Local CCFs, comprised primarily of volunteer citizens appointed by county boards of commissioners, are partners with the PSCCs in developing local plans for crime and delinquency prevention. This CCF initiative is "a revolutionary form of governance bringing individuals, communities, non-governmental organizations and federal, state and local government together to identify community strengths, concerns and opportunities; develop comprehensive plans and share the responsibility for implementing those plans; and, share accountability for results" (Oregon Commission on Children & Families 1996).

The initiative embodies a strong belief in the "wisdom and will of local communities to make good decisions about the health and safety of children and families" (Oregon Commission on Children & Families 1996). In several Oregon counties, the CCFs have pioneered innovative approaches to enhancing community wellness and safety, including "community progress teams" that galvanize citizens to make a difference in their own home communities (Marion County Children and Families Commission 1996). The CCFs have also developed new ways to define desired outcomes of prevention and intervention efforts and methods of measuring progress toward these goals that are both objective and practical (Pratt et al. 1997). The Deschutes County CCF is the only one in Oregon that has been given the authority, by the board of commissioners, to review and make recommendations on proposed budgets of all county agencies providing services and resources for children and families.

Oregon is a national leader in implementing community policing and victim advocacy programs. Many Oregon law enforcement agencies now emphasize localized problem-solving and preventive activities, encouraging collaboration and mutual accountability between police and citizens. Both the Bend Police Department and the Deschutes County Sheriff's Office have implemented community policing programs. Concern for victims of crime has long characterized Oregon's approach to justice system issues. One of the first victim services programs in the United States was founded by the Multnomah County (Portland) District Attorney's office nearly 20 years ago. The state attorney general's office operates a victims' compensation program, and CASA (Court-Appointed Special Advocate) programs currently serve nearly all Oregon counties, including Deschutes. Convened in 1994, the Oregon Domestic Violence Council encourages localities to develop community-centered, collaborative processes, including their own local domestic violence councils, "to create change at the local level for seemingly intractable problems" (Oregon Domestic Violence Council 1996).

Countervailing Policy Trends

Recent changes in Oregon's sentencing laws, state juvenile corrections system, and taxation policies have limited the discretion of local decision makers and placed constraints on resources available to implement community justice principles. Despite these shifts, community justice has continued to flourish in Deschutes County, in part because the state legislature authorized the county to pilot test some of the key concepts of community justice (see "The Evolution of Community Justice" below).

In 1994, Oregon voters endorsed Measure 11, a sentencing initiative that imposes mandatory minimum prison sentences on all those convicted of specific crimes (assault, robbery, sex offenses, kidnapping, manslaughter, attempted murder, and murder). Juveniles 15 to 17 years old charged by the district attorney with these crimes must be tried as adults, and the minimum sentence for the least serious of these offenses is 5 years, 10 months, without consideration for probation, early release for good behavior, or parole. This measure has resulted in a prison population explosion, requiring the state to devote an increasingly large proportion of its budget to prison construction and operation and correspondingly reducing the funds available to counties for prevention and education initiatives.

In 1995, the legislature created the Oregon Youth Authority (OYA) to operate state facilities for delinquent youth and funded a significant increase in bed space available to incarcerated adjudicated juvenile offenders. OYA has regionalized its operations, placing new secure facilities in areas of the state that are remote from the formerly centralized state facility. With increased capacity closer to more counties and the promise of more and better treatment and skill-building programs for inmates, the new OYA facility system may have the unintended consequence of encouraging counties to securely confine more youth who are not dangerous but simply troublesome.

Statewide property tax initiatives passed by voters in 1990 and expanded in 1997 severely limited county taxing authority and made the state legislature responsible for funding public education. Although this is arguably a more equitable method of funding schools, it also expands state government's influence on local education policies and practices and places education budgets in direct competition with expenditures for prison operations and construction.

Deschutes County Characteristics

The form that community justice takes is affected by the context in which it evolves, so it is important to highlight the characteristics of Deschutes County that likely have influenced its community justice initiative. The county's climate and geography influence population growth and density, which in turn have significant social, economic, and cultural impacts.

Located in the heart of Oregon, Deschutes County encompasses the snow-capped Cascade Mountains and the fertile valley, range, and forest-lands of the high desert country or Central Oregon plateau. Bend, the county seat, is 160 miles from Portland, 343 miles from Seattle, and 490 miles from San Francisco. The average elevation of the county's principal towns is 3,525 feet. Its annual precipitation is 12.04 inches of rain and 33.8 inches of snow. The average temperature in January is 30.5° F., and in July 62.5° F. French-Canadian fur trappers of the old Hudson's Bay Company gave the name Riviere des Chutes (River of the Falls) to one of Oregon's most scenic rivers, from which the county of Deschutes took its name. The county was created from a part of neighboring Crook County in 1916. County borders were generally determined by how far a messenger on a horse could ride in one day's time.

Deschutes County has experienced the most rapid growth of any county in Oregon during the past 10 years, largely due to its invigorating climate, which provides year-round recreational opportunities for skiing, fishing, hunting, hiking, climbing, biking, boating, golf, and rockhounding. People also choose to settle in the county to enjoy the benefits of rural or small-town life. The county has become a magnet for active retirees who have a strong interest in sustaining the quality of life that drew them to the area. Portland's newspaper, the *Oregonian*, recently published an article titled, "Laid-Back Bend Draws Rat-Race Refugees," which suggests that the city's 34% growth in the past seven years can be attributed primarily to an influx of affluent professionals "who have decided that work means more than just making money and that retirement doesn't mean putting their feet up" (1999, B6).

The county is not ethnically diverse. In 1993, Portland State University (PSU) estimated that nearly 98% of the county's residents were Caucasian, 2% were of Hispanic origin, and less than 1% were either Native American, Asian/Pacific Islanders, or African American. More than one-third of the county's population resides in the city of Bend; other main cities are La Pine, Redmond, and Sisters. According to the Center for Population Research at Portland State University, Deschutes County's population is presently nearing 110,000, a 30% increase in the past seven years.

Central Oregon Community College's main campus is located in Bend, with seven off-campus teaching centers throughout the region. The college provides comprehensive course work at the freshman and sophomore levels for transfer students as well as training and retraining programs in business, industry, the trades, and government service. Three public school districts serve Deschutes County.

The county's principal industries are tourism, retail trade, secondary wood products, recreational equipment, aviation, and computer software. The cost of living in Bend is slightly above the national average, whereas the average family income in the county is slightly below the statewide average (Central Oregon Economic Council 1999). Observers feel that there is a significant and growing disparity between the income of the wealthiest and the poorest county residents. Though the Bend airport is served by several major airlines, no public transportation system is available in Bend or any of the other major towns in the county. This presents particular challenges to those without access to private vehicles, particularly youth, the elderly, and the economically disadvantaged.

Though it is likely to continue to grow, Deschutes County will remain small enough to make countywide change more feasible. However, the issues and challenges facing the county are complex enough to require that successful change processes be thoughtfully designed and implemented. The county has been working for years to build a community-focused justice system that can mobilize citizens to invest in the health and safety of their communities. Community leaders feel that the potential for fully implementing community justice in Deschutes County is great.

Community Justice in Deschutes County

Oregon's commitment to local control, community-based corrections, community policing, and victim services provides an environment supportive of Deschutes County's pioneering efforts to establish restorative and community justice strategies and programs. With the support of influential state legislators from Deschutes County and its elected board of commissioners, the county has crafted statutes, enacted resolutions, and leveraged resources empowering it to implement its community justice vision. Because of its long tradition of community activism, innovation, and collaboration in social policy making, Deschutes County continues to lead the way in "placing the community and victims at the center of justice activities and efforts" (Barajas 1997).

The Evolution of Community Justice

The evolution of community justice in Deschutes County has been both planned and serendipitous, the product of considered and sustained actions combined with a fortunate confluence of circumstances and opportunities. County leaders have collaborated for years to lay the groundwork for a new approach to juvenile offenders and at-risk youth, envisioning a community justice system in which prevention of crime would be the county's highest priority. Those juveniles convicted of crimes would be held accountable for repairing harms they cause and would also have access to a full range of education and skill-building opportunities. Nearly all youths sentenced to a period of secure confinement would be held in county rather than state facilities.

County leaders see communities, including individual crime victims, as the primary customers of the justice system. The leadership also envisions that a broad spectrum of community members will become active partners with justice and other agencies in preventing and responding to crime. Public and private agencies are encouraged to work together to build a seamless continuum of services and support for all children and families. County and community leadership continue to weave these strands together to create the fabric of community justice in Deschutes County.

Practicing Balanced and Restorative Justice

In the 1980s, Deschutes County developed community corrections programs that make it a state and national leader in the balanced and restorative justice movement (Klein 1996). Its juvenile department was one of the first in the United States to adopt the "balanced approach," in which public safety, offender accountability, and competency development are considered equally important goals of the justice system. By 1996, the Board of Commissioners adopted a resolution creating a unified adult and juvenile Department of Community Justice, and by June 1997, the department had commissioned all juvenile probation officers as community justice officers.

Other justice system agencies share the Community Justice Department's focus on the needs and perspectives of crime victims. The Deschutes County District Attorney's office "attends to victims' needs

---

COMMUNITY JUSTICE RESOLUTION

Whereas, the citizens of Deschutes County should be entitled to the highest level of public safety, and

Whereas, increasing rates of juvenile and adult crime pose a threat to our citizens being and feeling safe, and

Whereas, a comprehensive crime reduction strategy requires a balanced emphasis on crime prevention, early intervention and effective corrections efforts, and

Whereas, the participation and restoration of victims should be a central responsibility of the criminal justice system, and

Whereas, Community Justice embodies a philosophy that engages the community to lead all crime prevention and crime reduction strategies,

Now, therefore, the Deschutes County Board of Commissioners adopts Community Justice as the central mission and purpose of the County's community corrections efforts. Furthermore, the County hereby creates a Department of Community Justice to replace the Department of Community Corrections.

BE IT RESOLVED that the Department of Community Justice shall work in partnership with the County's citizenry to carry out effective crime prevention, crime control and crime reduction initiatives.

BE IT FURTHER RESOLVED that the County shall construct a Community Justice Center to provide facilities and programs for victims of crime to be restored, for offenders to be held accountable and to gain the competencies to become responsible and productive citizens and for the community to have access to an organizational center for a broad range of crime fighting efforts.

DATED THIS 25th day of September 1996, by the Deschutes County Board of Commissioners

from the time a crime is reported to the time the last restitution payment is made," and the Circuit Court "has placed a particularly high priority on victim-offender mediation" as a principal means of resolving nonviolent cases (Maloney 1998). The Community Justice Department provides ample opportunities for juvenile offenders to repair the harms their crimes caused through direct restitution to victims or by participating in meaningful community projects such as Habitat for Humanity home building, cutting and distributing firewood to senior citizens, or pine needle clean-up in neighborhoods rated high risk for fires.

In 1994, voters passed a bond measure that enabled the county to construct a new Community Justice Center dedicated in June 1998. In addition to expanding local secure capacity for juveniles by 420% (from 10 to 42 beds) and serving as the home base for most community justice officers, this facility also provides office space for a wide variety of community agencies that focus on competency-building activities. It even houses a fully equipped dental office that enables local dentists to provide free care for children from low-income families.

Investing in Prevention

Providing adequate detention capacity for the county's juvenile offenders was necessary but certainly not sufficient to shift public safety investment priorities from intervention to prevention. So in 1996, county leaders proposed a Community Youth Investment Project (CYIP), which was enacted by the 1997 state legislature as HB 3737. This law, applicable only to Deschutes County for a six-year pilot period, 1997-2003, is a centerpiece of the county's strategy to implement community justice. The statute provides a powerful incentive for the county to use fewer state "close custody" beds for adjudicated youth by allowing it to invest any savings of state funds (attained by avoiding use of these beds) in local crime prevention activities.

As of October 2000, Deschutes County had reduced its use of OYA institutional beds by 72% from 1998 levels. As part of HB 3737, Deschutes County agreed to utilize only seven OYA close custody beds (a reduction of 16 from its previous use level) and to pay the state for any bed days used in excess of this cap. Between 1997 and October 2000 (34 months), the county has been at or under the cap 85% of the time. During this period, the county paid the state $19,098 for its use of 145 bed days in excess of the cap (Deschutes County Community Justice Department 2001).

Deschutes County has received a total of $1,711,497 from the state to fund the CYIP from fiscal year 1997 through 2001. About two-thirds of these funds have been used to house in the local detention facility juveniles who otherwise would have been sent to OYA institutions. By October 2000, 60 youth had completed or were participating in the local residential component of the CYIP. The program combines education, substance abuse treatment, family interventions, victim restitution, and community service to promote local accountability. Aftercare is provided to all those successfully completing the residential portion of the program. Eight of the participants (13%) were remanded or revoked to OYA for violations of program conditions. About three-quarters of those who successfully completed the CYIP residential program by October 2000 had one or more felony adjudications prior to their placement in the program, but only 7% of these youth had one or more felony adjudications following graduation from the program.

About one-third of CYIP funds have been reinvested in prevention and early intervention services that are intended to reduce the county's long-term need for corrections programs and facilities. In its January 2001 report to the state emergency board, the county states that it has "carefully selected and funded six early intervention and prevention programs that address the continuum of issues that prevent young people from leading productive and positive lives." These programs are as follows:

- For children from 0 to 7 years
    ReadySetGo. Between 1999 and October 2000, 30 parole/ probation families with newborns and young children received weekly home visits by parent partners and monthly home visits by public health nurses.
    First Step to Success. Between 1998 and October 2000, 76 acting-out or withdrawn kindergartners and their families have been provided positive behavioral and learning techniques that will enhance their school success.
    SMART. Recently added to the CYIP reinvestment plan, this will help provide mentoring and tutoring to K-2 children with reading difficulties.

- For children 8 to 18 years
    Community Youth Connections. Since 1999, 600 at-risk youths have participated in skill-based and positive relationship school activities.
    Quantum Opportunities. Another recent addition, this program is a high school graduation incentive program that is modeled after the national Blueprints concept.

- All ages
  Family Trax. A countywide parent training and education effort that involved 35 families between 1998 and October 2000 and reached thousands of other citizens with resource booklets and warm line support.

To fund these programs, Deschutes County uses not only CYIP early intervention funds but also a portion of the funds received through SB 555, a Juvenile Crime Prevention (JCP) package that became effective in January 2000. It provides all Oregon counties with resources targeted to address the needs of middle and high school youth (and their families) at risk of becoming chronic lawbreakers. Oregon counties were given discretion to develop their own plans for use of these funds within broad state guidelines, and Deschutes is the only county able to devote all of its SB555 resources to universal prevention and early intervention activities. Other counties used from 30% to 100% of their allocation for "basic services" (including shelter care beds, day reporting, and intensive probation supervision) for adjudicated juvenile offenders, options that in Deschutes County are subsidized by its CYIP legislation.

Deschutes County is clearly committed to implementing "comprehensive approaches to prevention [that] can build resiliency and reduce risk-taking behavior, thereby lessening problems like crime, alcohol and drug use and school failure" (Deschute County Commission on Children and Families 1998). For Deschutes County's community justice policy makers, this kind of crime prevention is the heart of community justice.

Engaging Communities and Citizens as Partners

Leaders of the Deschutes County community justice initiative are fond of saying that "nothing in nature grows from the top down." In this, they acknowledge that although strong and charismatic leaders serve as catalysts and provide momentum for the county's efforts, the seeds they plant require nurturing by the entire community in order to bear fruit.

Engaging community members in the work of community justice is one of the most challenging aspects of implementing community justice. Citizen mobilization requires a multifaceted approach that goes well beyond traditional public information campaigns (see Fulton 1998). In its Community Justice Resolution, the Deschutes County Board of Commissioners offered a vision of community justice in which communities "lead all crime prevention and crime reduction strategies."

Citizen engagement in community justice requires that government agencies, employees, and elected officials not only provide information about the goals and outcomes of community justice but also initiate and maintain a dialogue with a broad spectrum of citizens and communities. Policy makers must respond to citizen concerns and priorities and also provide opportunities for lay citizens to participate in community justice policy making. Government officials can encourage citizens and community organizations to provide resources and services in support of community justice activities, and they should provide meaningful recognition of the accomplishments of citizens and communities in community justice endeavors.

Because successful partnerships are built on mutual support and accountability, citizens and communities must in turn accept their fair share of responsibility for preventing crime and creating healthier communities. Citizens should stay informed about community justice concepts, goals, and outcomes and commit to working together with elected officials and public agencies to define and resolve problems. Community organizations and citizens have diverse energies, talents, and other resources they can contribute to this process.

Everyone engaged in the work of community justice must recognize that constructive change requires planning, patience, and persistence. Deschutes County has made considerable progress in engaging citizens and communities, and citizens have responded favorably to the call to work in partnership with county government to enhance the well-being of their communities.

Bringing Justice to Communities

Deschutes County's Public Safety Coordinating Council initiated efforts to address neighborhood needs and interests by developing teams of community police officers, community justice officers, and neighborhood leaders and residents that focus on cooperative efforts to improve safety and prevent crime. In a Bend apartment complex that was the source of many police calls for service, a Neighborhood Safety Team rented an apartment where community justice and police officers, along with staff from allied social service agencies, were available to residents. This apartment office became a place where residents and their children felt comfortable coming to share concerns and solve problems with professionals who were available and sympathetic to their needs. One result of this pilot effort was a significant reduction in police calls for service from the apartment complex. The increased trust between residents and criminal justice practitioners that was observed by many participants is less easily measurable but no less powerful. Funding problems have stalled expansion of this program to other locations, but its positive results are expected to propel further exploration of this neighborhood-based model of justice system service delivery.

The Merchant Accountability Board, which since 1997 has served as the victim board for shoplifting cases, is another example of bringing justice back to communities. The board is a group of merchants who volunteer to serve on a panel that hears and adjudicates referrals for shoplifting offenses. Between August 1997 and December 2000, the board heard 543 cases and developed contracts for restitution with all but one. Of these, 452 (84%) were either current with or had completed their restitution, and 90 (16%) were noncompliant as of October 2000.

Providing Information About Community Justice

Deschutes County leaders have explored a variety of ways to provide citizens with information about community and restorative justice, including the following:

1. Organizing a series of "Back to the Community" forums, which began in 1997 and were attended by hundreds of individuals who had the opportunity to hear about and discuss community justice issues and concepts

2. Sponsoring presentations by community justice policy makers and staff to a wide variety of local organizations

3. Leveraging the support of the Central Oregon Ad Club and other local organizations to produce a comprehensive media campaign designed to broaden awareness of services for families and children and recruit volunteers to help families in need (one of the slogans created by the Ad Club is "Kindergarten teachers have the ability to identify a child with a potential problem We all have the ability to identify a potential solution.")

4. Making use of Internet technology to provide citizens with ongoing access to information about the status of community justice efforts

As an Innovations in Government 2000 finalist, the county's CYIP program was awarded a $20,000 grant, which has supported public relations and planning for the next phases of community justice implementation. Deschutes County recognizes that keeping citizens informed about community justice initiatives is necessary but not sufficient to engage and empower them in the work of building healthy and safe communities.

Listening to the Public

Most citizens want to have a voice in government and want to feel that policy makers and community leaders are listening to their ideas, opinions, hopes, and frustrations. In addition to discussions at forums, which have by their nature involved only a select group of citizens, Deschutes County policy makers have utilized three methods to learn about diverse citizens' views and values:

1. A 1997 citizen survey asking how tax dollars should be used, and what types of sanctions and services ought to be utilized for offenders

2. Structured interviews with 85 community leaders and policy makers inside and outside the justice system, conducted in the spring of 1997, designed to ascertain their knowledge of community justice, its strengths and weaknesses, and what steps should be taken to make it a reality in Deschutes County (see Community & Justice Solutions for Deschutes County 1998)

3. A series of 16 citizen focus groups held in elementary schools, fire halls, and community centers across the county in the spring of 1999. The focus group consisted of approximately 15 grassroots citizens selected to represent viewpoints of diverse residents in each elementary school catchment area. Group members were asked to discuss their views on what strengthens communities, how they know when they are getting a return on their investments, and how they would be willing to contribute to making their community a better place to live (see Community & Justice Solutions for Deschutes County 2000).

In general, all these approaches have revealed that there is enthusiastic support for community justice initiatives and for the values of restorative justice. Deschutes County citizens and leaders are proud of their communities, are willing to invest time and energy in making them as safe and healthy as possible, and see community justice practices as the cornerstone of this endeavor. County residents are more interested in accountability than punishment of offenders and would rather invest in education than in-carceration.

Community leaders who were interviewed suggested that outreach to and active engagement of a broad spectrum of citizens must be a high priority for future community justice efforts. Focus group participants concurred, with many saying that they want to *know* that their opinions are being heard and responded to *and* that their actions can make a significant difference in quality of life for them and their families, neighbors, and communities. One of the intended outcomes of the focus group process is development of meaningful and measurable quality-of-life benchmarks that can be applied to determine where the county currently stands and what must be done to make its communities healthier and safer. In this way, what is important to citizens will form the basis for evaluating whether community justice is working in Deschutes County.

Citizens Engaged in Community Justice

Many Deschutes County citizens volunteer their time and talents to fur-ther the goals of community justice. Some of the more visible ways in which citizens are engaged are as members of a variety of local advisory boards, including the Commission on Children and Families, the Public Safety Coordinating Council, and the Merchant Accountability Board. Citizens also serve as volunteer mediators for the Victim-Offender Mediation Pro-gram (VOMP), CASA for abused or neglected children, sponsors of com-munity work service opportunities for offenders, mentors for at-risk children and youth, and caregivers for victims of crime and others in need of support. Many community members donate not only their time and expertise but also their financial and other resources for community justice work. Most of these volunteers say that their most important reward is knowing that their work has made a difference. The county also strives to recognize their efforts in a variety of tangible ways such as designating parking spaces at the Community Justice Center for the exclusive use of crime victims and volunteers.

More and more, citizens of Deschutes County appear to be recognizing that government cannot by itself make communities healthy and safe. Gov-ernment leaders and workers are working to inform citizens, to listen and respond to them, and to involve them in decision making as well as service provision. Still, there is much to be done if community justice is to be fully implemented, and *community governance* (i.e., broad citizen participation in *all* operations and policies of government) is to become a reality.

Current Status and Future Directions

Although the success of Deschutes County's community justice process must be judged in the final analysis by its results, assessment of its outcomes must be approached with caution, because "deeper learning often does not produce tangible evidence for considerable time" (Senge, Roberts, and Ross 1994:45). In other words, "You don't pull up the radishes to see how they're growing" (Senge et al. 1994:46). Moreover, many of the benefits produced by a "learning organization" and by successful community justice practice (e.g., enthusiasm, commitment, and cooperation) are very real but not easily quantifiable.

Deschutes County has remained true to its vision of community justice. Within the past few years, county leadership has largely succeeded in making prevention of crime the county's highest priority, putting in place a system to hold juvenile offenders accountable for repairing the harm they have caused while providing them with education and skill-building opportunities and securely confining youths in county rather than state facilities. Crime victims and communities have become the hub of the justice process, and a large number of community members are engaged as active partners with justice and other agencies in preventing and responding to crime.

Though some of the factors contributing to these successes are not easily replicable outside Deschutes County or Oregon, many of the key ingredients are already present in other jurisdictions. Deschutes County's evolution illustrates how jurisdictions can build a community justice process by creating a climate of constructive change and taking advantage of opportunities for innovation as they arise.

Keys to Success

A number of factors likely have contributed to Deschutes County's success in implementing community justice principles and practices. Some are demographic, whereas others are grounded in community values and attitudes. Deschutes County's experience suggests that in the long run, successful transformation from traditional to community justice policies and practices must be built on a commitment to prevent crime rather than simply reacting to individual criminal acts (Barajas 1999). This does not necessarily require *more* societal resources but rather a *reallocation* of resources from punishing or confining criminals to restoring and nurturing healthy communities, families, and children. The keys to Deschutes County's progress toward community justice lie not only in its unique demographics but also in the values and vision of its citizens and the resources they continue to invest.

Demographics

Deschutes County's relatively small population size makes some aspects of planned change easier to implement, and its healthy local and state economy means more jobs and a more stable funding base for public and private sector initiatives. Many new residents come to Deschutes County with a commitment to preserving the quality of life that drew them and time and resources to invest toward that goal. Long-time residents are fiercely proud of their county and want to preserve its livability for their descendants.

Values

County leaders and residents value being pioneers and are willing to take risks and try new ways to resolve old dilemmas. They share a strong commitment to preserving individual dignity and autonomy and to valuing the contributions every person can make to the general good. Most community leaders and citizens believe that effective change grows from the grassroots, that is, from the efforts of citizens who are willing and able to take responsibility for the governance of their communities. Many citizens believe that they must provide energy and leadership in partnership with government in order to ensure that their communities will be safe and healthy.

Prevention of crime is seen by most county residents as the best and highest purpose of the justice system. When crime occurs, most agree that the focus should be on restoration of victims and communities through holding offenders accountable for repairing harms they cause and enhancing their competencies to become productive citizens.

Leaders and citizens understand that healthy growth takes time and requires persistence, patience, and a willingness to periodically take stock and retool in order to reap the greatest rewards. Citizens and their leaders believe that success in community justice or any other collective endeavor should be measured using criteria that articulate local priorities and values in measurable terms.

Resources

Deschutes County has charismatic leaders who motivate and inspire others to work toward community justice goals. The county's elected officials and representatives are actively supportive of community justice principles. Public and private sector staff of justice and other agencies serving families and children are dedicated and energetic. There is a large cadre of talented citizen volunteers who are engaged in policy making and service delivery efforts on behalf of their communities, neighbors, and families. The county has leveraged both public and private funds to support its focus on prevention and the restorative and community justice movement. Finally, information about the positive impacts of community justice on people's lives and on the quality of life in the county is routinely provided to citizens, staff, and policy makers.

Although Deschutes County is a unique tapestry of demographics, values, and resources, other jurisdictions possess many of these keys to successful implementation of community justice. Perhaps the most important factor that must exist is *hope*—that crime *can* be prevented, that citizens *will* invest their energies to make their communities safer and healthier, and that government *will* be accountable to citizens and communities for its part of the continuing effort to improve quality of life. With this vision, the journey toward community justice begins and is sustained.

Challenges Ahead

Deschutes County recognizes that community justice will never be "done"—it is a dynamic, ongoing process in which opportunities continue to arise and challenges must be overcome. The county has clearly accomplished much in the last five years of the millennium since resolving to implement community justice. The next set of challenges on the horizon encompass both contextual and strategic concerns that must resolved if its community justice system is to remain viable and flexible. Deschutes County leaders and citizens are aware of these issues, and have begun to address most of them.

Context

Although the influx of affluent retirees has been an economic boost for the county, its rapid population growth is also placing strains on infrastructure, human services, and the natural environment, which threaten to erode the quality of life dear to its citizens. The increasing economic disparity between the most wealthy and the poorest citizens may undermine efforts to build consensus around the best approaches to improving quality of life.

Strategic Issues

Though charismatic leadership is a tremendous asset in moving community justice forward, Deschutes County must continue to expand its leadership circle to encompass a larger number of individuals capable of motivating and inspiring others. One of the keys to successful implementation of community justice is developing partnerships—between citizens and government workers, between professionals in different agencies and areas, and among diverse groups of citizens. Deschutes County has built networks of partnerships in many arenas, but much more work remains to be done to formalize and expand these working relationships.

Resistance to change is human nature, particularly when one's power or security appears to be threatened. Deschutes County must address directly the concerns of those, professionals and others, who fear that implementing community justice will, at best, be just another set of bureaucratic hoops or, at worst, render them obsolete.

The frontline staff of all justice, human service, health, education, and treatment agencies must be engaged as partners with leaders and citizens in the community justice process, just as the juvenile justice staff have been since the mid-1990s. As with citizens, this requires providing them with information, listening and responding to their concerns, and inviting them to help design strategies and approaches to make community justice a reality in the county.

The restorative and community justice principles that have been put into practice with the county's juvenile offenders and their victims should be expanded to include all adult offenders and their victims. Effective intervention with adult offenders can break the cycle of dysfunction that too often results in their children becoming dropouts or delinquents.

Deschutes County should build on its successes by continuing to collaborate with other Oregon counties to expand community justice initiatives within the state. Though Deschutes County has gained legislative support for its work, statutory and fiscal support would likely be more stable over the long run if other counties join with Deschutes in advocating for community justice principles and practices.

The county should thoughtfully articulate its overall action plan or blueprint for implementing community justice, so that individuals, agencies, and organizations may understand better how their strengths and talents can contribute to positive change. Serendipity can be exhilarating, but only by planning and providing a structure for everyone's efforts can the county effectively harness all the powerful creative energy so apparent among its citizens and government workers. Deschutes County's leaders must continue to reach out to citizens through a wide variety of means, providing information, listening, responding, and inviting them to become actively engaged in making and implementing community justice policies.

In medieval Europe, creating a beautiful and functional tapestry required the labor of many who worked over a long period of time within the framework of a grand design. Weaving an effective community justice system out of diverse values and multifaceted priorities similarly requires an articulated vision, many hands, and an enduring commitment by all to realize its promise. Deschutes County exemplifies a community justice process that is evolving to encompass all agencies of the justice system as well as community partners and citizens. This small, politically conservative county thinks big, acts on its values, and learns from its missteps. With an open and inclusive public engagement process and thoughtfully designed but flexible community partnerships, the capacity of Deschutes County communities to ensure justice, health, and safety for all citizens will continue to grow. The county's experience can also help guide other jurisdictions that are committed to implementing community justice concepts and processes.

References

Barajas, Eduardo, Jr. 1997. "Community Justice: Bad Ways of Promoting a Good Idea," *American Probation and Parole Association Perspectives,* Summer:16-19.

———. 1999. "Changing the System for the Right Reason", *Texas Journal of Corrections,* September.

Bucqueroux, Bonnie. 1996. "Community Criminal Justice: Building on the Lessons that Community Policing Teaches." Pp. 8-14 in *Community Justice: Striving for Safe, Secure, and Just Communities,* edited by E. Barajas. Washington, DC: U.S. Department of Justice, National Institute of Corrections.

Central Oregon Economic Council. 1999. *1998 FactBook.* Retrieved August 7, 2001 (from www.coedc.org/factbook.htm).

Community & Justice Solutions for Deschutes County. 1998. *Perspectives on the Community Justice Process in Deschutes County, Oregon.*

———. 2000. *Community Justice in Action: Deschutes County, Oregon.*

Deschutes County Commission on Children and Families, Community Justice Work Group. 1998. *Reinvestment Plan and Priorities: Building a Healthy Community: Investing in Prevention.*

Deschutes County Community Justice Department. 2001. *Deschutes County's Community Youth Investment Program (HB 3737): Report to the State Emergency Board.*

Etzioni, Amitai. 1996. *The New Golden Rule: Community and Morality in a Democratic Society.* New York: Basic Books.

Fulton, B. A. 1998. "Mobilizing the Community." Pp. 87-110 in *Community Justice Concepts and Strategies,* edited by K. Dunlap. Lexington, KY: American Probation and Parole Association.

Klein, A. 1996. "Community Probation: Acknowledging Probation's Multiple Clients." Pp. 23-29 in *Community Justice: Striving for Safe, Secure and Just Communities,* edited by E. Barajas. Washington, DC: U.S. Department of Justice, National Institute of Corrections.

"Laid-Back Bend Draws Rat-Race Refugees." 1999. *Oregonian,* October 3 1999, p. B6.

Maloney, Dennis. 1998. "Justice and the Community." Pp. 209-214 in *Community Justice Concepts and Strategies*, edited by K. Dunlap. Lexington, KY: American Probation and Parole Association.

Marion County Children and Families Commission. 1996. *Update from the Community Progress Teams.* Author.

Oregon Commission on Children & Families. 1996. *System Development and Implementation Framework*."

Oregon Domestic Violence Council. 1996. *A Collaborative Approach to Domestic Violence*. Salem, OR: Author.

Pratt, C. C., A. Katsev, T. Henderson, and R. Ozertich. 1997. *Building Results: From Wellness Goals to Positive Outcomes for Oregon's Children, Youth, and Families*. Salem, OR: Oregon Commission on Children and Families.

Senge, Peter M., Charlotte Roberts, and Richard B. Ross. 1994. *The Fifth Discipline Fieldbook: Strategies and Tools for Building a Learning Organization*. New York: Doubleday.

Chapter Seven

Afterword

In the Shadows of Community Justice

Shadd Maruna

> Between the idea
> and the reality
> Between the motion
> and the act
> Falls the Shadow

"The Hollow Men," T. S. Eliot*

Probation is dead. At least, that is the verdict of numerous, recent reports on the state of the art in community corrections. For instance, Maloney, Bazemore, and Hudson (2001) argue that probation has "gone the way of the Edsel" in terms of performance and reputation, and like the Ford Company's infamous failure, probation needs to be retired. Most important, they not only advocate the end of traditional probation

*Excerpt from "The Hollow Men" in *Collected Poems 1909-1962* by T. S. Eliot, Copyright 1936 by Harcourt, Inc., Copyright © 1964, 1963 by T. S. Eliot, reprinted by permission of the publisher.

practice (which they say is based on the "rather bizarre assumption that surveillance and some guidance can steer the offender straight") but also dispensing with the "brand name" of probation (which they rightly argue is a vague and uninspiring term). Echoing the authors in this collection, they suggest that a more fitting mission and name for probation should be *community justice*. Indeed, community justice as an ideal has been the subject of considerable excitement and theoretical examination over the past two decades.

Yet just what this new ideal might mean in reality is never entirely clear. Stanley Cohen (1985) warned that "community" is a "magic word" that "lacks any negative connotations" (p. 117) and "rolls off the tongues of correctional administrators . . . as easily as . . . radical community activists" (p. 36).

> It would be difficult to exaggerate how this ideology—or, more accurately, this single word—has come to dominate Western crime-control discourse in the last few decades. . . . Almost anything can appear under the heading of "community" and almost anything can be justified if this prefix is used. (p. 116)

The contributors to this collection, therefore, provide a crucial grounding to this conversation by sketching a rough geography of community justice in practice. Clear and Karp began their trilogy of books on community justice by describing community justice as an "emerging field" with diverse origins and (grass) roots (Karp 1998). This book was followed by the outlining of a coherent, theoretical picture of community justice in *The Community Justice Ideal* (Clear and Karp 1999). At last, with this third book in the series, we have community justice in action. Uneven and scattered, from Ventura County to Vermont, these case studies provide a first glimpse into the lived reality of community justice, warts and all.

Implementing an ideal—especially one as lofty as community justice—is never easy. Yet, it is in the shadows between ideal and practice that community justice can best be understood. It is essential that the lessons these case studies provide be heeded and that these pioneering experiences take a privileged position in the discussion about community justice and the future of probation.

Although the editors call this the third volume in a trilogy, I strongly doubt that the series will end here. The next volume will likely investigate the question of outcomes. In the end, does all of this stuff seem to work? Does community justice make a demonstrable difference? We live, after all, in a time of great reliance upon assessment, efficiency, outcomes-based management, and empirically proven best practices. The question of the hour in corrections is, "What works?" (Martinson 1974)—as well as, "What doesn't and what's promising?" (Sherman et al. 1998). For most, this means measuring outcomes and empirically demonstrating success.

Still, as is obvious from the contributions to this volume, the practice of community justice is still in its infancy. It would be premature to begin drawing conclusions about the viability of this paradigm based on these early experiments. As Lin (2001) and others have pointed out, "What works?" may be precisely the "wrong question" to ask at this point in time. Before we can understand and interpret outcome data, we first need to understand the implementation process. The urgent question in regard to community justice is not "What works," but "Can it work?" and, if so, "How does it work?" After all, we cannot assess the success or failure of community justice ideals before we figure out just what community justice involves or what seems to be going on under its guise.

Moreover, as with any true paradigm shift, assessing the success of community justice enterprises will require the development of new "lenses" (Zehr 1990) and new methods of evaluation. Within the framework of community justice, the question of "What works?" takes on entirely new meanings, and previous evaluation criteria may no longer be appropriate. In particular, community justice calls into question the evaluation fraternity's reliance upon changes in recidivism rates as the be-all and end-all of programmatic success.

Interestingly, Robert Martinson, the father of the "What works?" question in correctional research, might have been among the first to foresee the need to transcend this technical definition of success in order to salvage the credibility and legitimacy of the correctional enterprise. Arguing that "the day of 'recidivism-only' research is over," Martinson (1976) argued

> The public [is] demanding some substantive knowledge about how to reduce crime and all it gets . . . is the dry crust of "middle base expectancy" and interminable intramural bickering about the esoteric mysteries of research design and significance tests and such-like oddities. . . . My neighbors in the 20th precinct [of New York City] are mystified. . . . "Show us a method for reducing crime or get out of the way."

Community justice theory insists that the perceptions of these neighbors be taken seriously and not dismissed because they are out of line with expert definitions of effective practice. As such, assessing community justice will involve far more listening than previous evaluation paradigms. Listening to community members. Listening to victims. Listening to offenders. And listening to community justice pioneers like those profiled in this volume. These voices and their stories—lurking in the shadows between romantic, community justice ideals and the cold, hard data of the "What works?" enterprise—are where the real community and real community justice will likely be found.

References

Clear, Todd R., and David R. Karp. 1999. *The Community Justice Ideal.* Boulder, CO: Westview.

Cohen, Stanley. 1985. *Visions of Social Control.* Cambridge, England: Polity Press.

Karp, David R. 1998. *Community Justice: An Emerging Field.* Lanham, MD: Rowman & Littlefield.

Lin, Ann Chih. 2001. *Reform in the Making: The Implementation of Social Policy in Prison.* Princeton, NJ: Princeton University Press.

Maloney, Dennis, Gordon Bazemore, and Joe Hudson. 2001. The End of Probation and the Beginning of Community Justice. *Perspectives* 25(3):22-30.

Martinson, Robert. 1974. "What Works? Questions and Answers About Prison Reform." *Public Interest* 35:22-56.

———. 1976. "California Research at the Crossroads." *Crime and Delinquency* 22:180-91.

Sherman, Lawrence, Denise Gottfredson, Doris MacKenzie, John Eck, Peter Reuter, and Shawn Bushway. (1997). *Preventing Crime: What Works, What Doesn't, What's Promising.* Washington, DC: U.S. Department of Justice.

Zehr, Howard. 1990. *Changing Lenses: A New Focus for Crime and Justice.* Scottsdale, PA: Herald Press.

Index

About the Editors

David R. Karp, PhD, is Assistant Professor of Sociology at Skidmore College in Saratoga Springs, New York, where he teaches courses in criminology and criminal justice. He is also a member of the New York State Community Justice Forum. He is the author of more than 30 academic articles and technical reports and 2 previous books—*Community Justice: An Emerging Field* and *The Community Justice Ideal: Preventing Crime and Achieving Justice* (with Todd R. Clear). Currently, he is engaged in a qualitative research study examining Vermont's community reparative probation boards. He conducts research on community-based responses to crime and has given workshops on restorative justice and community justice nationally.

Todd R. Clear, PhD, is Distinguished Professor of Criminal Justice at the John Jay College of Criminal Justice of the City University of New York. He has served as president of the Academy of Criminal Justice Sciences and as vice president of the American Society of Criminology. He is the author of more than 100 academic articles and 9 books. He is interested in community justice, the impact of incarceration on community life, and the role of religion in justice policy and practice.

About the Contributors

Joanna B. Cannon is a PhD candidate in the School of Criminology and Criminal Justice at Florida State University. Her primary research interests include community justice, mediation and dispute resolution, juvenile delinquency, and the juvenile justice system.

Ronald P. Corbett, Jr., PhD, is Executive Director of the Massachusetts Supreme Judicial Court. Prior to assuming that position, he worked for 26 years for the Massachusetts Probation Service and held the position of deputy commissioner for field services at his departure. He has been a member of the graduate faculty at the University of Massachusetts/ Lowell since 1991 and has published widely in the areas of corrections and management.

Jodi Lane, PhD, is Assistant Professor of Sociology in the Center for Studies in Criminology and Law at the University of Florida. She is a member of the RAND research team evaluating the South Oxnard Challenge Project. She is the editor (with Joan Petersilia) of *Criminal Justice Policy*, and her recent articles have appeared in *Crime & Delinquency* and *Federal Probation*. Her interests include juvenile justice policy, corrections, fear of crime, and program evaluation.

Teri K. Martin, PhD, is the proprietor of Law & Policy Associates, a consulting enterprise specializing in juvenile and criminal justice strategic planning, policy analysis, program development, and evaluation research.

She also participates in Community & Justice Solutions, a multidisciplinary consortium of justice, education, and human service professionals dedicated to supporting the evolution of community justice locally and nationally. She serves her Oregon community as chair of the Washington County Commission on Children and Families and as a member of the county's Public Safety Coordinating Council. She received her PhD in Public Policy Analysis from the University of Illinois at Chicago.

Shadd Maruna, PhD, is Lecturer at the Institute of Criminology at the University of Cambridge, Great Britain. He is the author of *Making Good: How Ex-Convicts Reform and Rebuild Their Lives*, which received the 2001 Michael J. Hindelang Award from the American Society of Criminology. He is currently working on a new book looking at the process of ex-convict reintegration.

Susan Turner, PhD, is Associate Director for Research and head of the Sentencing and Corrections Center for RAND Criminal Justice. She has conducted studies on racial disparity, private sector alternatives for juvenile offenders, work release, day fines, 14-site nationwide evaluation of intensive probation supervision, drug courts, and sentencing and correction alternatives for drug-involved offenders.

Evelyn Zellerer, PhD, is Assistant Professor in the School of Public Administration and Urban Affairs at San Diego State University. Her publications on restorative justice, especially with respect to indigenous peoples and violence against women, have appeared in the *International Journal of Comparative and Applied Criminal Justice*, *International Review of Victimology*, and an edited book, *Restorative Community Justice*, by Gordon Bazemore and Mara Schiff. She is interested in gender, culture, social justice, and qualitative methodology.